FINDING AUTHOR SUCCESS

FINDING
AUTHOR
SUCCESS

Discovering and Uncovering The

Marketing Power Within Your Manuscript

DEBORAH RILEY-MAGNUS

2011

ireadiwrite Publishing Edition

This ireadiwrite Publishing edition is published by arrangement with Deborah Riley-Magnus, contact at writerchef@sbcglobal.net

ireadiwrite Publishing - www.ireadiwrite.com

First print edition published by ireadiwrite Publishing, a division of Central Avenue Marketing Ltd.

FINDING AUTHOR SUCCESS:
Discovering and Uncovering The Marketing Power Within Your Manuscript

ISBN 978-1-926760-66-7

Published in Canada with international distribution.

Cover Design: Natalie Preston

Cover Photography: © Tomasz Sowinski © Pavlo Vakhrushev courtesy iStockPhoto

To authors everywhere.

FINDING AUTHOR SUCCESS

CONTENTS

INTRODUCTION

At the age of forty and after a lucrative twenty-year career in advertising, marketing and public relations, I decided that it was time for a change. That career had served me well but I'd grown tired of the back-biting, negative aspects of it so of all things, I decided to become a chef. I went to culinary school, worked physically harder than I ever had in my life and loved every moment of it. After graduating, I was a salad girl, then a line cook, a sous chef and finally an executive chef and through it all I parlayed what I knew of the advertising biz to market both myself and whichever restaurant or banquet facility I worked for. Over ten years I found terrific pleasure in that career – hot, grueling and tiring as it was – until one day a few herniated discs chose to end it. This five-foot-nothing woman with back problems could hardly lift those three gallon stock pots any longer and I chose to return to my original secret love, writing.

Back in culinary school, I learned a few vital things that work in just about any career a person could find themselves. I learned to always use the correct tool for the job, and if I didn't have it, to create something that would work. No four inch cookie cutter? The top of a cleaned, empty tomato soup can works just fine. I always had with me a cool spoon I found in my grandmother's kitchen drawer. It had a very pointy tip and was perfect for drizzling just the right amount of sauce for my plating. I learned to always carry a ruler in my knife bag because inevitably, I'd need to measure something perfectly, and I discovered that layering flavors and textures created the best recipes. But the most important lesson I ever learned came from Chef Chuck Baux, my favorite chef instructor at school. As we all stood like deer in the headlights and terrified to begin our first assignment in a professional kitchen, he simply raised an eyebrow and looked at us over his specs. "It's only a meatball," he said. "Some ground beef, eggs, cheese, bread crumbs and spices. Roll it and cook it. Not brain surgery, only a meatball."

These days I'm an author and an author success coach. I layer old and new concepts with unique and proven ideas for platform building, promotion and publicity. The goal is to create the best possible solutions for author success, no matter how the author is published. Books don't just sell themselves in this crazy time within the publishing industry. Author support from publishers has greatly diminished and it's time for you to step up to the plate. Anything is possible – but only if one looks for the possibilities.

I want you to think about that meatball as you approach this book and begin to create your own effective author success strategies. It may seem daunting and scary but really, it's not brain surgery. It's only a meatball. Get all your tools and ingredients together and begin the journey into planning your successful career as an author.

Part 1

CREATING AN EFFECTIVE BOOK BUSINESS PLAN

"I'm a tidy sort of bloke. I don't like chaos. I keep records in the record rack, tea in the tea caddy, and pot in the pot box."

~ George Harrison, The Beatles ~

PUT ALL YOUR DUCKS IN LINE

Let's begin with a statement every author should already know. Writing a Book Business Plan is as important as writing your book. Why? Simple.

- Writing is a business
- Writing is YOUR business
- Nothing reminds a business person of the importance of their business more than a business plan

With a strong plan – a living, breathing plan that organically grows with your manuscript, the ever changing publishing landscape and always vacillating market – you will not believe how far ahead of the game you can really get. A well prepared Book Business Plan includes the following:

- The Perfect 25 Word Pitch
- Market Exploration
- Selling the Sizzle
- Exposure and Promotional Plans
- The Elusive Budget
- Author Platform and Book Platform
- Understanding Professionals
- Tools for Focus

Let's start off on a strong note: we're going to get down and dirty to make you and your book stand apart then lure in those fans and readers. But before you move into the process for creating a successful author career, you need to get all your ducks in line so we're going to begin with an assignment. I know, I know, you're saying "homework already?" But think about this. What bank would give you cash to start a business if you didn't have a logical way of explaining what that business will do? They need to see a well-developed business plan, and it's what you need in order to stay on track as your business moves ahead and grows. It controls your trajectory and alerts you to off-track activity or trends. You're going to begin the same way any good business plan is put together. It may seem sophomoric, but you would be amazed how many authors keep vital information scattered in their mind, somewhere on their desk or on the note pad beside their bed. The time has come to be business-like. Compile all these elements into one folder. If you don't have them all at this time, make a note to get them done soon; having your arsenal sharp and full and polished is the name of the game. Here we go:

- Book title, genre, length, fiction or non-fiction. (If some of this information is not yet determined, use guesstimates)
- If non-fiction - a completed book proposal
- A 25 word elevator pitch, a 250 word pitch, a 2 page synopsis and a 5 page synopsis of your book
- Target reader demographic information
- Pitch strategy (if already represented by a literary agent, note the agent's strategy. Why? Because you should know how your agent is pitching your work.)
- Author Platform strategy to date
- Book Platform strategy to date
- Author group affiliations
- 5 year goal and 10 year goal for success
- Creative inspirations, images and thoughts that drive you

Now, putting these important elements together in one place will do two important things. It will make you realize how important it is to see – physically SEE – how well you know your project, and it will help you understand how your project interlaces with the career success plan you have in mind.

Use an accordion folder, a desktop folder on your computer, a file drawer, a collection of yellow lined pads, a bound journal, a milk crate, whichever works best for you but put it all together. If you can't locate any single

MISE EN PLACE

[Meez ahn plahs]

A French term referring to having all the ingredients necessary for a dish, prepared and ready to combine up to the point of cooking.

BEST EVER MEATBALLS

1 lb lean ground beef

2 ea eggs

¼ c grated parmesan cheese

2 T minced onion

1 T minced garlic

3 T dried bread crumbs

2 ea cloves minced garlic

6 ea large basil leaves, chiffonade (rolled & chopped into thin strips)

Mix all ingredients. Roll into two ounce balls. Sauté and serve with tomato sauce. Makes 8 meatballs.

AUTHOR SUCCESS

1 well planned Book Business Plan

1 author with extraordinary creativity and courage

1 well written book

4 meatballs (for stamina)

piece of information quickly, you're adding minutes, probably hours, months or years to reaching your goal. This information will vacillate and improve, swell and get sharper as you move ahead, but unless it's all in one place, how will you know?

Authors work in many ways to create their book. Some meticulously plot, others make mind maps or colorful charts, some even move into a dream-like fantasy world to explore character development and dialog. Why should creating your Book Business Plan be any less creative or thoughtful? It's a work in progress and really great Book Business Plans have built-in contingencies to cover many possibilities. Getting your ducks in line is a way of solidifying the reality of what you want to see happen.

THE PERFECT 25 WORD PITCH

25 Words from Query to Sales Success

Now we're going to have some fun. You've heard it a thousand times – if you can't tell someone what your book is about in 25 words, you simply don't know it. Of all the items listed earlier for your ducks file, finding the perfect 25 words to explain your book is the most important, and the most difficult. If you can't do this, you're not ready for the next step. You're not ready to pitch or query or even consider joining a serious critique group, much less promote the book. That's how important this is.

These 25 words represent the seed for everything. It will determine how far you're willing to go with creative promotions and platform building, how hard you'll push to create demand for future books, and how succinct and clear you're going to be with not only your writing, but your overall strategy for author success. In essence, those 25 words will, without a doubt, be the cornerstone for your success. Your assignment is to write your 25 word pitch. In those few words, you need to convey the following:

- Who will relate to your book? (The target demographic)
- Why must an agent represent your book, publisher publish it, or reader buy it?
- The genre of your book? (If non-fiction, the specific subject and reader interest)
- What is your book about?

Note the order of importance. The description of your book – that thing authors feel is most important – falls fourth in line. There's a reason for this. If an agent or publisher is willing to take a risk on you, they need to know you understand the market where you'll be trying to sell that book. They're not the creative entities here, they're the businesspeople. You need to show them that you are too, and get that message across in 25 little words.

That's a lot to pack into so few words, but this is an extremely important task. Twenty-five words is nothing more than a hiccup to describe your book but in truth, if you can't spit out an effective description this brief, you don't really know your book's true market or how you need to promote it. Too much emotion comes with those long, excited descriptions that authors love to spout. This task will force you to look at your book as the product. It's a widget. What does it do and who will use it? Don't fret, just sit down and start writing. You're no stranger to editing, so plan on doing a lot. It doesn't matter if it's 24 or 27 words or exactly perfect yet.

Chances are, as you progress through this book, your 25 word pitch will evolve, become tighter, brighter and more powerful. Right now it may take on one form, as we go along, it will shift.

Ah - but when it's perfect it's golden, and those few words will serve you well for a very long time. This tiny "blurb" will be the meat of everything from queries and pitching your book to agents and/or publishers, to explaining it to the media when seeking interviews. It's the perfect beginning for a perfect sound bite. It will easily explain your book to venues for book events. It will be the core of your press release campaigns and serve as the basis for your book video. It is the polished answer to the question – So, what's your book about? It will make your book stand apart and above the others, but only if done well. Never forget, it will also change subtly when necessary, the way women alter eye makeup and shoes from day to evening activities. It will be versatile but solid as steel. Believe it or not, this is the key lesson of this entire book.

A well designed Book Business Plan is a living, breathing thing built on 25 simple, perfect words. The Book Business Plan can be nurtured along with your book's development, or be designed after the book is finished. It can and should be flawless in its flexibility whenever and however necessary to attain the objective. If your plan is too tight and has no room to grow or breathe, it will die an ugly death and take your career with it.

Here are a few not-so-good and good examples to get you started.

Not-so-good Example #1, Fiction

Gabrielle's Travels: A young woman discovers magical stones on her property that send her into the past where she meets the unsavory ancestors she never knew existed.

Critique
Who will relate to this book? Women? Young adults? Children?

Why must an agent represent it, a publisher publish it, or reader buy it? No clue, there's not enough here about the target market or story to justify the risk.

The genre of this book? Chick lit? YA? Women's fiction? SciFi adventure? Supernatural? The genre is completely unclear and thus, so is the market.

What is this book about? We know a bit about the story, but do we really care about those stones?

Good Example #1, Fiction

Gabrielle's Travels: Gabrielle MacFee meets a handsome widower, discovers her family's witchcraft history through unwanted time-travel, and learns that love can not only save her, but make her whole.

Critique
Who will relate to this book? Women.

Why must an agent represent it, a publisher publish it, or reader buy it? It has a unique twist with time travel, witchcraft and romance – all marketable.

The genre of this book? Romance, sub-genre: paranormal.

What is this book about? The story is much clearer here than in the not-so-good example and far more relatable.

Not-so-good Example #2, Non-Fiction

Finding Author Success: Understanding how to market, promote and create effective publicity is difficult for all business people, but most especially for authors seeking publication and sales for their books.

Critique

Who will relate to this book? Authors, but why do they need a book on this subject?

Why must an agent represent this book, a publisher publish it, or reader buy it? There a thousand books out there about marketing, promotion and publicity. Why would there be a need for another one?

The specific reader interest? Business/Self help

What is this book about? Nothing new or of special value

Good Example #2, Non-Fiction

Finding Author Success: In this turbulent publishing landscape, authors who can't create book sales, no matter the genre, format or publishing venue, will lose. This is the success blueprint.

Critique

Who will relate to this book? Authors seeking success

Why must an agent represent this book, a publisher publish it, or reader buy it? This book speaks to a new niche market in need of targeted assistance to find sales success

The specific reader interest? Authors and publishing industry professionals, business/self help seekers

What is this book about? Clearly this book is about addressing the unique marketing, promotions and publicity needs of authors in the current publishing climate.

Query Punch

What's a query? I'm sure most of you are conjuring up horror images of investigating literary agents and/or publishers and filing rejection letters, but a query is far more than that. As an Author Success Coach, I often hear the worst of the worst from my authors. They talk about how many times they've been rejected by agents or publishers but they haven't taken a close look at those numbers.

Here's the real truth: your book has not been rejected by a literary agent or publisher unless they request a portion or all of your manuscript, and then reject it.

Think about that. In this particular case, a query is in the form of a letter, meant to be clean, clear and concise and tell the prospective agent or publisher what your book is about. A good query letter will get requests (unless of course you have not queried the correct agent or publisher for your book genre). Your book is not being rejected if they never asked for it. It's your query letter that's being rejected.

What does that mean? It means you're not being succinct or powerful enough. You're not opening your query correctly, or you really don't know what your book is about because you can't say it in a few punchy words. This is an extremely important skill, because even if you never send a query letter, even if you self publish and bypass all the pitching and querying connected with finding publication, you still must query.

You query reviewers to review your book. You query book clubs to read your book. You query unique sales locations. For example, just because your book is e-published doesn't mean you can't appear in unique venues. If your book is a mystery about murderous old-lady gardeners, you can query gardening blogs, clubs and websites for an opportunity to post your book and sales link on their websites. If your romance is about a character who loves shoes, you can query shoe store and designer clothing websites for a chance to advertise or post your book cover and sales link.

You query libraries for a chance to speak about your book or your writing skills during meetings or teaching opportunities. You query interest groups live and online to participate in promotional events. You query book talk radio and television programs for the opportunity to promote your book.

Queries are everywhere in an author's life, so best get the most punch you can.

The only way to effectively query anything regarding your book is to perfect and know your 25 word pitch intimately. You should be able to recite this pitch in your sleep. Remember, you never know when or where you'll get a chance to do a pitch. Imagine that the independent book store owner in town is holding a book symposium and he's right there in the elevator with you. If you want to be part of his event, you better know how to pitch him without a second thought. Unless that elevator stalls, you've got precious few moments to make an impression.

There's magic in knowing your perfect 25 words, but there's also magic in knowing where and when and how you can use them.

This tiny collection of the perfect 25 words will serve for everything from:

- Pitching your book to agents and/or publishers
- Pitching it to the media when seeking interviews
- Explaining your book to venues for book events
- The core of your press release campaigns
- The perfect advertising tag
- The perfect dust jacket blurb
- The powerful sound bite

And there are hundreds of other ways to use your perfect 25 words, you just have to look for the opportunities. Expand the power of these words and press the boundaries of what you can actually accomplish by being the really good writer you are. Your perfect 25 word pitch shows confidence in knowing that your query letters, no matter who they're going out to, are clear and powerful.

Power Press Releases

Now we're going to talk about press releases. Again, not what you think. Yes, you use these perfectly crafted 100 - 250 word letters (sound a little like queries?) to get the media to notice you, want to talk about you, interview and write about you. But oh, the lowly press release has so many other uses.

Exactly what is a press release? Simple. Who. What. Where. Why. And when. Nothing more and nothing less. Let's break it down.

- Who – That's you, the author. Everything you want them to know about you and your expertise, qualifications or accomplishments. How you can be reached and where they can learn more.
- What – This is where a press release gets very specific. See, a press release must be news. So, the what might be about your soon-to-be launched book, or your launch party, or the fact that your book is sponsoring an event to raise money for a related charity.
- Where – Simple, if the release is about your book being launched, you will tell them where the book can be purchased. If the release is about a launch party or fundraising event, you give the location. If your book is only available in ebook format, you will list the online locations for purchase and give them the buy links.
- Why – This is where you get deeper. Are you a first time author? Are you having a party because it's your first book? Fifth book? You're kicking off a series? Are you supporting a charity and why? You must state the why that makes this news.
- When – Dates. The date of the party or event, the date of the release. The date when books will be available. When means when and no, you can't just skip this one.

These items do not need to appear in order, but if even one of them is missing, unclear or lightly passed over, the whole press release is not correct. News people can smell ambiguous information a mile away. They also want information in a quick, brief blast. That way they can effectively decide if it's worth their time to pursue more.

I learned a strong economy of words years ago when I began writing radio and television commercials. Did you know that a 60 second radio commercial is 150 words and not one word more? A 30 second radio or television commercial is 75 words and no more. And those limited number of words must carry the vital information: company name, phone number and sometimes the hours of operation. Tight, huh? And you thought 25 words was hard.

A press release should actually never be more than a single page (although some major corporations do much longer releases, there is a tolerance level of courtesy offered IBM that you and I will never see from the media). There's a strict format.

- Total word count (including headline): 100 – 250 words
- Left top: The words - For Immediate Release
- Right top: Contact name, title and phone number (on three flush right lines)
- Centered, all Caps: The Headline (make it punchy!)
- Body: Always open with a dateline which is simply the date and city of your released information. The body should be double-spaced, straight forward, crafted cleanly and informative. You must repeat the contact name and phone number, and when the press release is finished, the line below, centered, must have three hash marks (###) or the number 30 with a dash before and after it. (- 30 -)

That's it. No fancy language, no frilly teasers, no vague insinuations. Not too dry and never too flowery. Just straight news information. Here's an example of a not-so-good and a good press release.

A not-so-good press release might look like this:

"CALLING ON AN ANGEL" LAUNCHES

Dateline, January 12, 2011. New York City: Today, first time novelist Mary Smith, announced the launch of Calling on an Angel, a psychological thriller published by XYZ Publishing. The book can be found on Amazon and in selected bookstores across the country. A launch event is scheduled for Friday evening at the CrossRoads Independent Book Store in New York City at seven PM. For more information contact Mary Smith through her publicist, Katherine Jane at Jones Publicity, (098) 765-4321.

# # #

A good press release might look like this:

"CALLING ON AN ANGEL" EXPLORES AUTISM

Dateline, January 12, 2011. New York City: Author and psychologist, Dr. Mary Smith, announces the release of her psychological thriller sure to take the bookshelves by storm. Calling on an Angel is a spectacular novel developed around the twisted dreams and actions of twin autistic youths who, while living in a parallel world all of their mutual making, save victims and become heroes. This emotionally charged tale explores the hope and possibilities surrounding the great strides being made to prevent and treat autism by a powerful internationally funded consortium.

A portion of all proceeds from the sale of the book will go to Autism Research. To attend the book launch event scheduled for Friday, January 16 from 7-9 PM at Manhattan's beautiful CrossRoads Independent Book Store on 54th Street. Please call for reservations (123) 456-7890.

# # #

Which one appealed to you? The first press release is as correct as the second. It covers the basics, the who, what, where, why and when of making an announcement but does it tickle your desire to learn more? Too-flowery releases can be easily discounted as not believable, but a bland release is more likely discounted as unimportant. Finding the balance is the goal.

The second press release strides the middle ground comfortably. It explains the book, the author, the charity affiliation and the event details. You'll also notice that this book's 25 word pitch is right there in the second press release version, giving the release far more impact.

So, why write a press release format at all? Writing in a press release format is a great way to learn how to communicate the "hard news" and "information" side of your book. It looks, feels and sounds professional. It makes your book more than the gushing, excited banter from your heart. It makes it solid.

Now, let's talk about this press release. Besides sending it off to all the appropriate media contacts, what else can you do with it? You can email it to everyone you know. You can use it as an event announcement for your various reading and writing groups. If you belong to online groups that have a connection with your book's plot – for example, Calling on an Angel might have a strong following with Yahoo groups and various angel and/or autism chat groups or email groups – this is a perfect announcement to post there.

Now print it. Stick it up on the bulletin board at your hair dresser, dentist office, vet, grocery store, community center and coffee shops.

What happens to you and your book when you write a press release format (aside from the obvious, which is that you intend to approach the media), is that suddenly you get a different kind of respect. If you do this right, people will actually believe you have a publicist. Perception is everything. Believing you are successful means people who may not have thought twice about you will buy your book and talk about it. Creating a real buzz can seriously move into a big arena if you are able to put together a good press release.

Later, in section #3, Tantric Publicity, we'll talk further on creating press contact lists and planning effective press campaign strategy.

Sound Bites that Bite Harder

What is a sound bite? It's the most basic comment you can possibly make with the most impact you can create. A sound bite can and should be (okay, now you're really going to hate me) as few as 10 words.

To explain this a little better, I want you to imagine that you're standing in a receiving line

---

OVERHEARD

The following is an exchange overheard in a Hershey Pennsylvania hotel during the Pennwriters Conference a few years ago. True story, I'm the one that overheard it!

Agent in elevator: "What's your book about?"

Excited author: "A guy who falls into a deep hole, breaks his leg and starts to bleed to death. He tries to use his cell phone but it got broken in the fall. He tries to scream but it hurts too much because he probably broke a rib or two, I'm not sure. Then he starts talking to himself. After that he's on a plane – "

Agent in elevator (desperately watching the gauge above the door): "Uh – huh, so he got out of the hole."

Excited author: "Yes, his mother had a premonition and sent a friend to get him. Anyway, he's on this plane and it's about to crash and – "

Agent in elevator (ready to leap out the moment the door opens): "What's the genre?"

Excited author (calling behind the exiting agent): "It's a really wonderful, well written humor/adventure/literary/maybe romance kinda … hey … do you want to represent it? Mister?"

---

with a hundred other authors. Those other authors have written books in different genres, in the same genres and in sub-genres. They've written non-fiction, how-to books and memoirs. Some of them are top ten best selling authors and some of them are first-time authors.

Now, moving along this receiving line in front of you and all the other authors is a long line of reporters. They are walking slowly, reaching out, briefly shaking your hand and they need to keep moving. That means you have mere seconds to get your sound bite out of your mouth and into their heads. It has to hook there so that when they get past all the other authors, they remember what you said.

This is an important lesson. No matter how unique your style or novel is, you are up against thousands of other authors for the readers' attention, discretionary dollar and loyalty.

Walk around any book store or browse Amazon's book screens. How many other books are listed or stacked on the shelves with yours or where yours will be? How many other authors write the same genre? Now imagine every one of those books on the shelves or all those lovely covers on the Amazon pages are shouting a 10 word sound bite at you at the same time. Which one are you going to hear and which one are you going to remember?

How do you stand out? How do you get attention? And how do you compete? Here's some homework for you.

Part one – Take your 25 word pitch and make it shorter by half, no more than 10 – 15 words. These 10 – 15 words must tell your story with impact and command. The listener must get a glimpse of the genre and want to know more.

Part two – Take one of your favorite books by another author and write a 10 – 15 word sound bite for that book.

The reason for this exercise is that as a reader, you are truly getting only what the author wanted you to get from their book. You haven't known this author intimately, he/she hasn't told you what they wished was in the book or what they removed from the book or even what they hope you'd understand about the book. All you know is the book. What you write as a sound bite for that book needs to come from the point of view of the reader.

You should be able to do the same thing with your own sound bite as you did with the other author's sound bite. The trick is to step away from your book, from the emotions of it and the love for it and simply punch hard with the most effective elements that tell the story. You can do it for books you read, and in order to really make your sound bite explosive, you have to be able to step away and do it with your own book too.

> *"There's nothing like looking, if you want to find something. You certainly, usually find something, if you look, but it is not always quite the something you were after."*
>
> ~ J.R.R. Tolkien, Author, Lord of the Rings ~

ASSIGNMENT

1. Now that you've faced the fact that editing your book wasn't the end of editing, write down your current 25 Word Pitch. Does it clearly convey the following vital information?
- *Who will relate to your book? (The target demographic)*
- *Why must an agent represent your book, publisher publish it, or reader buy it?*
- *The genre of your book? (If non-fiction, the specific subject and reader interest)*

- *What is your book about?*

Remember, these 25 words will tighten, become sharper and even change for a second or third version as you move along in your marketing, but the main elements MUST be present.

2. Write your query letter (even if you've already queried and gained representation and/or a publisher, you must do this exercise). Be sure to use your 25 Word Pitch within the query and keep the letter as tight and clean and informative as the pitch. This will serve for a number of purposes down the marketing road but always remember, even a good query letter must be flexible enough to shift slightly for whoever will be reading it.

3. Build the bones of your press releases, making sure that the who, what, where, why and when elements are covered. Be sure to have your pitch appear as a prominent feature of the press release whether it is number 1 or 101 in a press campaign. Be flexible and never forget to mention the contact name and number twice.

4. Now jot down at least three different 10-15 word sound bites. These are your perfect go-to Tweets, the neat push on Facebook, the lovely line for your email tags and book signing flyers or posters. Changing them up serves various target markets and keeps the idea fresh for you and your fans.

5. And finally, sit and make a list of all the possible uses for your 25 Perfect Word Pitch. Be extremely creative. Would it work on a business card? As a screen saver? Maybe even on your answering machine message? Have fun with this and keep in mind, when the Perfect 25 Word Pitch is on the button, it conveys everything you need to get someone to ask, "Hey, where can I buy that book"?

MARKET EXPLORATION

It's time to take a stab at Market Exploration. Who are you writing for? What do they look like? Where do they live? Where do they buy the books they read? In an independent book store? At the big chains? Wal-Mart? Amazon? How do they like to read and enjoy their books? Hard back? Paperback? Ebook? Audio book?

Let's go further. Where do they learn about the books they like to read? Is your prospective reader viewing book videos? Does s/he check *The New York Times* Best Seller List to find what they want? Do they frequent the library? Belong to book clubs and reading groups? Only purchase books recommended by friends? What kinds of books do they prefer and are you writing for them … or for you?

Big, confusing questions, but all important and serious. If you don't know your reader as intimately as you know yourself, you just may be talking to yourself and no one else.

Yes, a literary agent may sign you because they adore your style or idea and feel strongly that they can sell it, but never forget who they're selling your manuscript or book proposal to – publishers who follow the proven formulas for sales. Yes, you may have friends and fans who love your online work and follow your platform to the ends of the earth, but are they really the ones who will cough up the cash and buy your book? Say you've chosen the self-publishing route and bypassed a lot of the traditional publisher choices regarding your book's printing or distribution; you still must know your market.

Let's simplify this a little. Say you are a chocolate lover. Where do you go for your chocolate? As a chocolate lover myself, I'll happily explore this sweet path right along with you. I might start at the local convenience store where they display the popular candy bars. For something a little different, I'll go to the grocery store and check out the boxes of chocolate chip cookies or packaged brownie mix. Okay, maybe I'm not in the do-it-yourself or prepackaged mood and I want something a little higher quality. Look for me at the local bakery where they've got chocolate slathered éclairs and freshly made moon pies. All right, maybe I'm looking for something more classy and ready to step it up even higher. Godiva, yes.

Now, what I've just demonstrated for you is that a prospective buyer can be reached at a number of different places, wanting a number of different qualities but still desiring the same satisfaction for their sweet tooth. The only thing that hasn't changed is the fact that the person loves chocolate.

Translated, chocolate represents your genre or non-fiction book subject. The various venues represent your prospective buyer's place of preference for buying or learning about books, and the quality levels represent the buyer's moods and level of loyalty to you as the author or to your genre. This is called market branding and only you can control, expand, or define it for your specific book.

If you write romance you can write several specific sub-genres from historic romance to paranormal romance to sweet romance or hot erotic romance and still – if marketed correctly – can span a wide range of readership and create broad loyalty. You can carefully direct your target markets the way the big publishing houses do, starting with hardback to reach those who keep books on their shelves to re-read – then to paperback or soft backs for those who prefer to spend less and read on the plane, train or during vacations. You will schedule e-publishing exposure to reach the audience who prefers to screen read, then generate loyalty through aggressive social media and start all over again with the next book.

It's all fun and games when you play book format sports, but there are no games if you don't know your reader, because every detail about that reader represents your market and all the colors of it.

A NOTE ON E-PUBLISHING

E-publishing is not the future, it's here right now and before you know it, most books will only be e-published. It's not a matter of when, it's a matter of how soon. Industry experts are predicting that within two to five years, all books – except the classics and best sellers published by the huge publishers – will be e-published.

An author should not shy away from e-publishers, even if they are already traditionally published in hard book format. It's to their advantage to reach out and get that additional e-reader audience. Jump on the train early. Remember, an ebook reader is as loyal to an author or genre as a hard book reader and it's been demonstrated that they actually spend more on books than paper book buyers. Making a mark in that readership pool is only smart. Don't forget, just like the buyer standing in a bookstore, the cover is what gets an ebook readers attention first, so fight for good, exciting and clear covers for your ebooks.

Where to start? At the end of course. Take a bottle of water (and some chocolate) and go on a nice full day of exploring in any large chain or independent bookstore. Stroll the aisles and take notes. How many books of a specific category do they have on the shelves? How many people beeline directly to those particular shelves and how many patrons meander around until something catches their eye? We all like to think we're writing something that is so unique it's never been done before but if the kind of book you've written is not on those shelves, it's not going to have a current market. If you spend your research time in small independent bookstores or online, it will tell you the same thing. This is what readers are reading and buying. This is the market that exists, now where does your book fit into it?

Naturally you could research numbers for specific genres and non-fiction books online, but I highly recommend you do it live and in person. There's a strong understanding gained from watching the prospective buyer in the wild, doing their hunter/gatherer thing and making choices based on the touch and feel (and the dust cover blurb) of the chosen book.

Knowing your market is about knowing THE market, understanding it and facing the fact that changing it may take some doing. To build a new market for something unique, experimental and/or unusual, it takes a whole different strategy. For our purposes, it's most important to find that very clear vision of exactly who will read your book.

ASSIGNMENT

Spend some time out in the trenches. Go to big bookstore chains, the book sections in Costco, Wal-Mart and even the grocery stores, tour the independent book stores and take a walk through a library. You'll be amazed what you learn. Have fun defining your audience, and watch out for the sugar high if you're eating chocolate. Now take an online field trip through Amazon books. Discover what you can learn about the books in your genre, their popularity and price. Note all your findings and make your assessments of what the market is reading and what you are writing. Is it a good match?

SELLING THE SIZZLE

"But … but … I'm a writer, not a salesperson!"

Boy, if I've heard that once, I've heard it a hundred times. Yes you're a writer, an author, a creative problem solver for your plot and characters and boy you are good at it. Non-fiction writers are natural experts at clean, precise research and organization. So why is it when you're faced with the challenge of plotting or strategizing your own success as an author, you crumble and quake? There's no need, you know. Whether you gauge your success in the amount of money you make, the fact that your book is on a bookstore shelf, or that your long lost friends and foes from high school are forced to notice your success because your name is in the newspaper, it's important to you.

After all, it's just like writing: it will happen with planning (plotting), identifying your competition (the antagonist) and creating the perfect strategy (action).

Creative minds find the elemental properties of sales and self promotion either beneath them or terrifying, but that's just silly. Done correctly, you can take your real power – those amazing solutions you create for your stories – and simply apply it to yourself. That book is your baby. You suffered for it, coped with morning sickness and back pains, walked the floors with insomnia over it and cleaned it up a hundred times to make it presentable. In return, that child has rewarded you with hours of entertainment and beautiful misery. You have a bond with it, a connection that can't be broken. My questions are: Why would you send it off into the world without your support? And why would you trust others to promote and encourage it? Others – being publishers – who aren't even doing much in the line of author promotion anymore.

I wouldn't let that happen and neither should you. You have invested your passion and time, your energy and sleep for this book and whether you're new at this or a seasoned veteran, it is always vital to not only participate, but hold the reins for your own success. Okay, off my soapbox and down to business. Let's talk about sales sizzle!

"A bestseller was a book which somehow sold well simply because it was selling well."
~ Daniel J. Boorstin, 1914 – 2004, The Image

No disrespect to Mr. Boorstin, but bestsellers don't just happen, at least not in this publishing climate. An author has to step up and create every opportunity for their book to sell. Once upon a time, in an ideal world far, far gone, publishers did all the promoting. No more. The public has to be aware of the book, and that's your job these days.

I know what some of you are thinking. "Sheesh, I haven't even finished writing my book and this crazy woman is asking me to think about selling it. Gimme a break!"

Nope, no breaks for you. If you don't think about these things now, you will be way behind the game when you need them. As I've said before (and will probably say a hundred more times), your success hinges completely on growing a success plan as you grow your book. This may sounds strange, since many authors are not really positive what their book will be until it's finished. Genres have split into as many species as arachnids. Even non-fiction subjects require extremely targeted marketing, for example, sales focuses are based on specific, pinpointed situations, markets, products or services.

I think I just saw your eyes glaze over. It's cool. Trust me, this will be fun.

To help explain how to do this, let's take an imaginary murder mystery entitled Tropical Murder. For this example, (which works for fiction and non-fiction) we'll journey through the process that breaks ground for not only the author, but the book too. Here goes.

Tropical Murder is a novel in need of a success plan. It's a book about murder in the tropics and many scenes feature tropical fish, so the author has decided to pitch her (perhaps even unfinished) book to pet stores that sell beautiful tropical fish. This is a very aggressive idea designed to break a whole new venue for novels. The author has established that people who love tropical fish would enjoy her novel. The pet stores already sell books, so why not novels? The author begins to develop creative solutions to make this happen. Let's break down the project into practical steps.

Getting her book into a pet store may or may not be breaking an untapped market, but it may at least serve as a double bump for the author's book. After the book is published, maybe the prospective readers will have heard about Tropical Murder on Twitter, Facebook, from a friend or on Amazon, but seeing it where they buy their fish tank supplies, a place they never expected to see it, just may tip the scales. The goal with creating unique book-selling sizzle is to always seek ways to tip those scales in your favor. Here's how you do that. Let's imagine you're the author of Tropical Murder.

The first step is to put on your walking shoes and go look around. Explore every pet store you can find, independent and chains. Chat with the sales people and even the managers about what books they are carrying, why, and who they get them from. No need to seriously pitch your idea now, in fact, this would be a great time to say something like, "You know, when I sit in front of my tropical fish tank, it's so relaxing and I end up reading." Just let it lie there for now.

Next, you will research further. If the pet store is an independent, who owns it? Who makes purchasing decisions? If it's a chain, how do you contact the decision makers? Would this be a purchasing decision made by each manager or only through headquarters? Emails are as effective as phone calls for learning this information. No need to be cryptic, people are always requesting this kind of information and answers are always given.

If the store in question already carries fiction on their limited bookshelves, ask the decision maker how he chooses the titles to offer their customers. Some questions you may not even have to ask, once you've opened the conversation, the contact may just pour out what you need to know.

If the store or chain does not and has never carried fiction with their books, don't get afraid or defensive, simply ask why and let them explain. The answer may be as simple as they've never tried it before and that's the perfect in for talking about your book.

Next, now that you've made friends with owners, managers and large chain pet store personnel, begin to brainstorm an event, no matter how far in the future that event might be, get it into the mental machine now. It could be a book launch event complete with press releases naming the particular pet store. There could be joint promotional themes, like a discount on angelfish for everyone who buys a book or attends the reading/signing book event. Let your imagination run wild. Create connections between your book and pet stores. Perhaps you can have fish tank skimmers placed inside the book as a free bookmark. Maybe you can go as far as have some tropical fish food imprinted with the title of the book. Have large posters made for the store windows and a banner (which you will need anyway for future events) featuring the book title.

The point of this fishy example is to help you understand that no matter how odd or off the wall an idea seems, it probably can be done. Imagine a major book event at the local pet store?

IN PRACTICE

Author Pamela DuMond discovered that the strategy outlined above could be very lucrative. After her comedic mystery, Cupcakes, Lies and Dead Guys was released, she did the exact cyber walkabout suggested.

"Connecting with baking communities is the most successful marketing effort I've made so far. I wondered if cupcake baker websites would like a funny book about a baker with a pinch of psychic ability. What I found was a wonderful fertile ground for promotion. There was no issue with promoting 'Cupcakes Lies and Dead Guys' at their websites because there was no competition for customers. A win/win!"

The author sells and signs books, does a reading and gets exposure because this will catch the local media's attention and of course, the author has sent out press releases with details of the event. Imagine the happy pet store owner. He's gotten more customers into his store on one Saturday afternoon than ever before and his sales staff has a chance to sell more pets and fish. Now imagine his competition. Trust me, they'd like the author to come do the same thing for them. Now the pet store business owners and managers are notifying their customers that the author will be there. Now the author has an image connecting Tropical Murder and its subsequent books with an all new market.

One more thing to imagine – now your book is being ordered by pet and tropical fish stores all over the country. Neat, huh?

New venues are great, but never forget, traditional promotions are just as important as the crazy promotions. You still must connect with libraries and bookstores, must seek out reviews, have an active blog and website for your book, be present at writing, authors and book shows with books in trunk to continue to promote, promote, promote, and maybe you should even bring the star of the show everywhere you go and have a fish bowl on the signing table with a beautiful tropical fish to greet everyone.

Being successful in this shifting publication and sales landscape isn't about doing what everyone else does, better than they do. It's about doing what everyone else does, better than they do and doing something really interesting above and beyond.

The Sales Sizzle for Tropical Murder – the only murder/mystery book tropical fish lovers (a proven large target market you've already researched) can buy in their favorite pet store.

Tropical Murder might be just as successful as any other book coming out this year without the added difficulty of finding a new market but hey, we don't want to be just as successful, we want to be more successful.

Now, what if Tropical Murder is sold only as an ebook? Ebook authors need to think inside the box – the computer box that speaks to cyber lovers who prefer to screen read their books at their PCs or on their e-readers. We start with the same premise, that tropical fish lovers will love the book. Now, where are these tropical fish-loving ebook buyers? Online, of course.

It is always a curiosity to me when an author feels they're at a marketing or promotional disadvantage because their book is e-published. Let's break this down simply.

Tropical fish stores have websites, right? Tropical fish lovers have chat boards and blogs about travel or snorkeling, right? Stores that sell snorkeling gear and travel arrangements to exotic parts of the world for the sport have websites, right?

Are you getting my drift? You are already floating around the cyber world daily on Twitter and Facebook and following sites and online shops and chat forums about your interests. Now it's time to take a cyber walkabout. Why can't you get your book sold on the snorkeling shop's website? How about sporting store websites? Travel agencies that specialize in tropic vacations have websites. Guest blog on the snorkeling or tropical fish lovers' blogs. Breaking ground for new sales markets for e-published books just may be easier than doing it for a hard cover book. You just need to swim in a different sea to find the possibilities.

Exposure and Promotional Planning

Attention! Attention! We just love attention, but only the best kind. It's a scary proposition, putting a few hundred pages of your soul out there for the world to see. But even more daunting than that is the prospect that maybe no one will look. Shiver!

Fear not, that's what we're here to talk about. There are a million tricks out there to perk a prospective buyer. You've seen it all, from "wall-to-wall carpeting bait and switch" to "test drive and get tickets to the All-Star Game". Just like car dealers and carpet companies, you are in business. Your product is your book. There are classic and bizarre ways to attract attention and draw your readers, but whatever you do it must point favorably to the bottom line – sales.

Getting attention for your book can require nothing more than a fantastic cover, or it may require something special to tip the scales. Let's explore deeper. Let's talk a bit more about helping you and your book stand out.

Fiction – Suppose you've written a novel about an amnesiac woman whose life is saved by a werewolf on a self-destructive mission to end his own life. You know you've got a great twist and wonderful story but you also know that there are hundreds of supernatural romances on the shelves and you must find a way to draw attention to yours. Solutions abound, sublime to absolutely ridiculous, but because you're aware of the importance of getting attention, you examine them all. For example, your book cover could be fur. You might include a CD collection representing the music your supernatural hero used to help the heroine recover and hold her memory: Their Songs. You may even develop a folded map to be inserted in the book that shows the route your main characters trekked during the adventure. If the book is e-published, even better, as downloading music, a program or map is even more reasonable.

Non-Fiction – Now, let's imagine you've written a non-fiction how-to book about the care and maintenance of a person's social media image. Of course you've done all the homework, researched deep and hard and already know that your subject is something people want and need to know. You've even presented it in a creative and entertaining way. Now what? To the drawing board. Should there be a downloadable program available to assist with the information? Maybe an attached workbook that helps the reader implement your advice?

Fiction and Non-Fiction – Strange opportunities for promotions present themselves even after your book is published. Honestly, what book really needs imprinted mugs or tee shirts to boost visibility? The book is already on the shelves, real or virtual, and frankly ladies and gentlemen, it's too late unless the book kicks off a series and those tee shirts will help build image and branding, or unless of course the book is about the popularity of promotional tee shirts.

ON SUPPORT

A thought on support … of course you have it: your friends support you, your family supports you and other authors support you. But there are times in this process when you realize that some of these vital groups don't support you in the ways you'd hoped. There's no point in wasting the energy to resent or be angry with these people. They simply don't understand the process of writing, becoming an author and remaining an author. Don't be discouraged when you discover that no, hubby just doesn't really care what you write or even that you write. Never feel slighted when your siblings repeatedly forget to read your book, and stay strong when your kids or friends become jealous of the time you spend at the keyboard doing your "writing thing".

This "writing thing" is important to you, and as much as you'd love the support of the special people in your life, sometimes you just don't get it. There is a solution.

Look elsewhere. There are local writers groups, online creative groups and if you can't find one that suits your needs, create one yourself. Call it the "Lone Authors" and schedule a monthly night out together for a few glasses of wine, book talk and the all important sharing of successes and failures.

Promotions and getting exposure can seem like really hard things to do. Writers are basically solitary creatures, living inside their imaginations and focused on telling their stories. Some hate to even leave the house. Out there is the black hole. Out there are distractions and time-sucking activities that steal away our precious writing time. But our prospective readers are out there, so what's a writer to do? I'll tell you what most authors do – Promotion, Publicity, and Procrastination. Let's take these three 'P's one at a time and explore them.

Promotion

Trust me, I've been in PR, marketing and promotions most of my professional life and this is a 'P' you simply can't ignore. I've seen it happen in every industry, not just the business of being a writer. It goes back to the nitty-gritty of being a professional.

The basics are the basics and these principals have been vital since the first cavemen convinced each other to trade shells and feathers for goods and services. If you don't tell someone you're an expert at something, how will they know? If you don't show them your skill, how can they decide they want it? If you don't promote, you basically don't exist.

Promotion is vital and it's vital early on in the process. As writers, we're all told to have a web presence. I have heard several people tell me that yes, they have a website for their book but it's basically static. Not good. You must update your site often, just like your blog. Granted, a blog may receive far more self gratification through responses and viewer numbers, but don't confuse numbers with creating awareness. Your website is where your creative juices get to really shine.

Update it at least once a month, more if possible with anything that works. If you write historic fiction, add a page that can feature your research techniques. Fantasy? Explore fantasy through the ages. Non-fiction? Talk about your subject like the expert you are, exploring different elements of it in each update. Update information as to where you are on your next book, or where to buy your current book. List where you will be speaking or signing your book and what events you'll be attending. Do small pieces on your characters, maybe even from their perspective, as though they're guest journalists. Be sure to put sample chapters up, more than a small excerpt. Hook those prospective book buyers in. Some publicists recommend as many as five chapters to hook your visitors. Make sure you have a 'contact the author' button so visitors can communicate with you.

Your website should NEVER be stagnant. It needs to be a living, breathing sales entity and you need to tell as many people as possible that there's something new to see there.

Another promotional tool is social networking to shout out your accomplishments, but always remember that social networking loses its power when all the viewer sees is you trying to sell your book. Be a person, make some friends, have some fun and your new found circle will be interested in knowing more. Treat the people you meet online like you would in real life, listen, find out about them, and then you can start to tell them about yourself.

Find additional venues to promote yourself and your work. Step outside the box. Find other websites to become visible on, sites that will host your sneak peek chapters. This is an opportunity to gain new followers from their fans. Share excerpts with other authors. Look for other authors to promote when you tweet or blog or update your own site. Friends help friends. It's a basic key to good promotion.

When do you start all this? Here's the kicker, you should have started when you got the idea to write a book. Honest. When an agent or publisher is interested in you, the first thing he or she does is Google your name. When was the last time you Googled yourself? It might be a good time to check your online presence by taking a look. If you have little or no presence, no matter how great your book is, you may discover that not only is an agent or publisher less willing to look at you seriously, but so are prospective buyers for your book. They just don't know you exist.

Publicity

Again, let's talk about basics. Let's say you have a product and it's not performing well. What do you do? It's like a failing baseball team who finds themselves in last place far into the season. The only thing that could be causing this is a failure to execute the basics well. A smart manager knows it's in the fielding, team dynamics, ball handling or attitude. He shifts the line-up and schedules more practices. He has his coaches work with the pitchers and he takes a look at the farm team for possible replacement options. He eliminates what doesn't work for techniques and adds players that do work.

Hope is never a good strategy. Just because your book gets published and available does not (unless you're Dan Brown or Charlaine Harris) mean it will simply sell. Promotion and publicity are hand-in-hand tools and must be used in tandem. Needless to say, if you haven't promoted the fact that you are a writer with a book for sale, publicity will not work as well.

Publicity requires a foundation on which to build. If you've adequately promoted yourself, you can get those platform slats and two by fours and start building. Publicity is the cannon explosion in Beethoven's fifth. It's the pinnacle of the build-up.

And like promotion, it has to start early. Like promotion it has to be creative and targeted, well thought out and rooted in the basics to help you succeed. Publicity isn't just a press release, it's a well crafted, exciting press release. A Publicity Campaign isn't one press release, it's a well planned series of press releases that feed the media excitement a bite at a time. Publicity is creating the excitement for your upcoming book. It's laying the groundwork for speaking or book signing events. It's telling the world what you have and making them salivate to read it.

A press release is designed to inform the media, but it works for so much more. Make sure you send your press release to every friend, relative and business associate you know, too. They need to be aware of your upcoming book launch. Sending them a press release makes them feel important and, you'll be surprised how many friends will take that release to the nearest book store and ask the manager to carry the book.

Publicity is about planning your exposure carefully and building the momentum and it has to happen before the book hits the real or ebook shelves. Done correctly, you may find yourself scheduled for live interviews or written up in magazines and newspapers. If you're super lucky, these events will be scheduled for immediately after your book is released. Done right, the promotion/publicity double team is unbeatable.

If you can't write a press release (and I doubt there's anything a writer can't write), take another look at the "Press Releases with Punch" section earlier. If you still don't feel confident about it, get a book. Guerrilla Publicity by Jay Conrad Levinsen, Rick Frishman, and Jill Lublin is fantastic but there are others to choose from. If you are adamantly against planning, writing and implementing your own publicity campaign, hire a publicist.

Either way, publicity is vital and can't be ignored if you want success. Making every venue or bookstore and every reader known or unknown who loves your genre aware that you have a book coming out is crucial. Period.

Procrastination

Buck it up. Don't procrastinate. Don't believe that if the book isn't in hand yet you have nothing to sell. Always remember, you are the product as much as your book. Creatively promote and publicize yourself now and your book will be successful. You can put off the laundry only so long before you run out of clean underwear. Treat your hard writing work better. Procrastination isn't a bad habit, it is a sin and can leave you with a failure. Stand up and shout now and get some well deserved attention. If you don't, no one will.

ASSIGNMENT

Make yourself a cup of tea or pour yourself a glass of wine then sit back and think hard.

Uncover at least three all new directions for your book marketing to go based solely on the content of your novel. The author of Tropical Murder, our imaginary book, found not only a new location to sell her novel, but a whole new audience and a way to reach them through pet store promotions. If your book is e-published, it's even easier to do these things online!

So enjoy the ride, see where it takes you and after writing down your three all new marketing directions for your book, get down and dirty and find ways to make them happen. Will it require money? Time? A new pair of walking shoes? Only you will know but if you do this well, you'll most likely be reaching a perspective audience no other author in your genre has even thought to approach!

THE ELUSIVE BUDGET

I know, I know. I've never met an author in the process of growing their success who has bulging pockets. We're all poor. So why talk about budget estimating or limiting costs? Because, even if your budget is $0, you must stick to it. How does a person do that?

Budget Planning for Success

What would you pay for? What have you paid for? Some authors pay large amounts to self-publish hard-cover books because they feel it's vital for their book to be seen on bookshelves. Some authors pay a technically savvy person to format their self-published ebook because they feel it's more important to get their book out there and sold than feel the weight of it in their hands. Some traditionally published authors with the big publishing houses feel that their publishers should do all the heavy lifting where promotions and marketing is concerned (poor, foolish authors who just may lose their future contracts with those big publishing houses if they don't take up the responsibilities and show exceptional sales). Some authors feel fine with doing something in the middle and some authors are just confused, scattered and worried.

What you do and how you do it has more to do with your plan than with your pocketbook. If you have a fantastic plan for success – a doable, rational plan that is aggressive and dynamic – but your pocketbook is empty, then you find the way to work around everything. Yes, I said EVERYTHING. I'm not talking about half-efforts either, I'm talking about finding paths to achieving your goals without spending a fortune. So, when I say you must plan your budget for success, the key word here is "budget", because you've already worked out the plan for success.

Let's take a basic plan element and break it out both ways, once for the wealthy writer and once for the not-so-wealthy one.

Let's imagine that you want a book video for your book. You can pay several thousand dollars for a professional, elegantly created, filmed, acted and edited book video by a real Hollywood producer. Or, you can create a book video yourself. (Of course there are other options in the middle, but for this exercise, let's look at extremes.) The difference is a ton of bucks, but the effectiveness can easily be the same if you know the reasoning behind a book video.

First, whether you or Cecil B. DeMille returned from the dead creates this book video, it still must effectively sell your book. In other words, (and this is my very strong opinion about book videos) your video should be no longer than 30 seconds. Not 45 seconds, not 3 minutes. 30 seconds. Why? Think about this. Everyone we know grew up watching television and a television commercial is 30 seconds long. We're basically programmed to shut off after 30 seconds. If you make me watch longer than that, I may not even reach the title of the book or the author's name, much less where I can purchase the book before I tune out. A successful book video is hard hitting, punchy and gets not only the story across but gives me a look at the cover of the book as well as where I can buy it. I clearly know the genre of the book and whether I'll like it or not in the first few seconds. The video will be clear and interesting enough to make me want to run out and buy the book or at least make a note to get it. Whoever creates your book video must understand your book intimately or you must know how to communicate the essence of your book briefly to that producer in order for the video to actually work effectively. Creating a book video, whether you or someone else does the work, gets very personal for an author and you must step away from that.

Like the 25 Words from Query to Sales Success section earlier, you need to get to the bare bones of the story, complete with genre and attention to the prospective reader to do a good book video. The point of a book video is to get the point of the book across. Doing it yourself might take you a little learning curve time and you can use the Windows Movie Maker program that was probably loaded onto your computer when you bought it.

These basic practices apply to everything from book videos to creating websites to developing promotional campaigns and planning your marketing strategy. Some things you may want or need someone else to do, other things you may do much better handling yourself. You know your story, just make sure you keep your emotional connection with it in check and you'll do fine.

Protecting Your Investment

Now that you've created a great book video or promotional plan or email network of prospective buyers, it's your job to assure that you use these things. Protecting your investments of time or money is more than just being paranoid that someone will steal your creative, it's about exposing them and using them so much that no one would dare steal them because everyone knows they are yours. The truth of life is that creativity is plagiarism with a flare. It's said that there are only five plots in the whole world and it's the creative author who breaks the mold with an amazing twist that finds success. It's the same way with everything else on the planet. Someone may imitate your book video or your website design but hey, if you've made sure your platform elements are totally focused on your book's unique "hooks" and reaching out to your specific targets, it won't matter. You will win sales and that's what this is all about.

Protect your investments by being extremely attentive to exposing your book video to as many of your targeted buyer lists, groups, networks and friends as possible. Do variations on your book video so that you can change things up occasionally and get more attention. The point of protecting your investments is to create such a vibrant buzz around them that you become synonymous with your platforms.

How to be Tempted the Smart Way

You must set a budget for several reasons, if nothing else, to control your trajectory. At most, to control your cash flow as it goes out the door. Here are a few words that should be burned into your brain as all the cool, exciting and tempting promotional concepts cross your eyes.

Free – First of all, nothing is ever really free, so always be watchful. Everyone wants something and if a professional or friend offers you something for free – time, a reading eye, suggestions or contact names – they will always want (and deserve) something in return. Field these opportunities carefully. Obviously you can't get every service you need to market your book for free, but you can make good use of those offerings of free help, as long as you have something of value to the person doing the offering. Are they secretly writing a book too and might they want your good eye as a reader? If they're stepping up to help with a book event, don't forget to ask what special events they might have coming up and offer to help. There's a mutual give-and-take that makes free services work. Never totally discount an offer of free service, but always look closely and consider the returned favor.

Cheap – Ouch, there is no uglier word in the budget language. Think about it. When something is cheap, it obviously is only a semblance of what it should be. It has holes or only works a short time, it functions only during the full moon or is only for left-handed users. When the price for a service looks too good, it usually is. Bait and switch is firmly planted in these offers too. Of course, you get what you pay for but hey, you can get so much more if you just pay so much more. If the service is significantly cheaper than the others, be a detective and find out why before you chance losing some of your precious budget.

Reasonable – Good word, reasonable. But what is a reasonable price for a promotional service? Let's take book videos again. Your genre and following have qualified this as a viable avenue for promoting your book. You've decided to hire for the service. How do you know the best price? Think value. Look at every site offering the service, write to the contacts at those companies, ask questions and never forget to inquire what additional services they offer that makes them better than the competition. Making a book video is cool, but what about marketing it? Does the company offer proven effective strategies for exposure of your book video? What is the added cost? How does it compare with other similar companies? Can you negotiate? Mix and match production/promotion packages? Does it fit in the budget? This takes some time but think about every element of this process the way you'd think about buying a house or a car. Reasonable is only reasonable if it has value.

Effective, High Visibility – Okay, this one gets a little complicated but let me simplify it for you. You have determined a budget. Let's imagine the overall marketing and promotional budget is say, $2,000 and not a penny more. How you use and distribute that budget should depend on your strategy. A high visibility strategy is very different from a targeted strategy. It's like shooting a bunch of pellets from a shotgun and watching them spray everywhere, or shooting an arrow aimed for the center bull's eye target. Both approaches work for their specific goal, but what is your goal? If you've chosen high visibility as your strategy, you'll need to be very creative and careful with your pennies. Look for every free exposure you can; from book reviews to setting yourself up as an expert on something within your book. Connect with groups focusing on that subject of expertise, be willing to get on a plane where ever you need to go and speak to these people. Promote yourself online, use your strong platform then, and only then, start spending your budget wisely. Press campaigns can be free or they can be expensive. Release services rage from $25 to thousands. Be aware of when, how and where these services distribute your release. Choose one that allows attachments (i.e. book cover, author photo, etc.) for when you need them. Only use a service that reports that the press release did in fact go out and how many contacts received them. Keep track of responses. Aside from a press campaign, budget for promotional campaigns. Is your book one that should have tee shirts and mugs? What will you do with them? Will you sell them on your website? Give them away at events? Are they creative enough to be successful? Will you purchase ads? High visibility means big exposure and while your book is waiting for publication, you need to be very vigilant about assuring that you are building a reading following that is waiting for the book. Keep in mind, you may need to expand your budget and hire a professional to assure your bucks get all the bang possible.

Effective, Targeted Visibility – Big difference here, and sometimes this is the most powerful way to build your following as it begins early and in your own back yard. You will focus your energies in your local exposure and expand it out. Speak at local book stores and libraries on your subject "hook", and belong to local related groups you can easily participate in (i.e. vampire and fantasy lovers groups, foodie groups, gardening groups, whatever relates to your book will work). Create your own "completely" free press release contact list by calling local newspapers, magazines, television and radio stations and finding the correct contact. Make sure they know your name, so that when you email press releases, they recognize you. Get visible everywhere. If your book is coming out soon, announce it on a simple flyer posted at your dentist's office, your vet's office, your insurance man's office, even on those local market and grocery store bulletin boards. Reach into your community and get some face time by helping with trash cleanup days or gardening days or even holiday local parades and picnics. It's the original social networking and it still works. Now you're all friends and it's no big deal to tell them you have a book coming out. Plan a big launch party and make sure you invite all your new friends in addition to the media. Celebrate the old fashioned way. Now, combine this with online social marketing. Reach your fingers out further and further with a really powerful blog (updated regularly), strong Facebook and Twitter presence and all along, keep building an email list. Notify all your subscribers of any news. Keep the excitement growing.

All this and you have yet to spend a penny, so plan your $2,000 strategically. Expand into purchasing broader press release services as you get closer to your book launch. Use your budget wisely. Choose the perfect professional to help you push through.

Avoid the Bad Juggling Act

Don't make the mistake of dropping one ball while trying out another. It's juggle time, and you can do it like an expert. Your platforms should move smoothly, be strategically and carefully scheduled and alive with activity. As you move further into the market and add promotional and marketing elements, nothing in your regular activities should be ignored. In fact, everything supports everything else.

For example, if part of your marketing strategy is to set up speaking engagements, book signing events, interviews on radio or television or online media, the first place you go is to your platform websites and blogs to begin announcing those events. Utilize your well established online and live social network activities. Keep those balls in the air because the minute you lose sight of one …

ASSIGNMENT

For this assignment I'd like you to get a clear idea of what works and what doesn't work for you and your book.

List everything you've seen on the internet or heard about from your author and writing friends regarding promotions, marketing and publicity services. Research each one carefully and jot a "YES" or "No" next to the services you like or don't like. Determine what you want to do to promote your book and start the process of fitting it into your budget. And remember, giving away a free book, even if it's an ebook, costs money – money you would have earned if that book sold, so be careful with your free promotional ideas. Only give away a free book if you KNOW it will add to the reputation of the book and word of mouth goodwill.

Your budget is elusive because it not only isn't formed, but it has no idea where to go. If you won a million dollars in the lottery today, what would you do? Would you go wild and buy every extravagant thing you could get your hands on? Or would you plan carefully where the cash would go, what purchases would have future value and how long you could make your money last? Some people would do one thing, some would do the other. Your budget is like winning the lottery. Don't blow it on low value services or imprinted mugs that may not serve your goals.

Create your plan carefully, list the services you like most and delegate your budget dollars to them then step back and look again. Do you really want to spend 50% of your budget on a book video? Does that advertising campaign by ABC Marketing guarantee to reach the number of possible book buyers you need? Is it vital to buy a plane ticket to a writer's conference for that marketing workshop when you can get it online for less than half the price?

Now get your eraser and start shifting your dollars around until you can step back and nod your head with a big grin, knowing you've figured out the absolute most effective way to use your budget.

AUTHOR PLATFORM AND BOOK PLATFORM

Let me guess, your first question is … Is there really a difference between an Author Platform and a Book Platform? And your second question is … Do I really need both? The answers are yes and yes. Let's explore the basics.

Author Platform

What is an Author Platform? Look in the mirror. It's you. It's all the elements that make you an author worth reading, no matter what you write. It's the promotion of the author you are and the author you want to be. It promotes you as the brand.

Recently an author asked about writing several genres and how to manage it. An Author Platform is what makes that not only possible, but functional and profitable. You see, if you have made you the brand, your book is just one of many kinds of books you will write. Hershey's Chocolates makes chocolate bars, Hershey's Kisses, Mars Bars all under the Hershey's brand. You, as a brand, can support whatever you churn out with smooth professionalism because you've made it clear to the world that you are an author, not just an author of romance or adventure or fantasy or YA or non-fiction or this title or that title. You are an author first.

How do you create an Author Platform? It's not easy but it's not so hard either. First, you'll need an Author Website that focuses purely on the career you're building. That's the place you keep an overall, easily downloadable media kit. That's the place you talk about ALL your work, what you're writing and what you're thinking about writing.

Making yourself a brand requires a clear focus on you as the author. An Author Website has an embedded blog with all things about the author, promoting them, showing their humanity through supported charities, and exposing them as an accessible "celebrity". It also has an effective, constantly updated and accessible Media Room.

Book Platform

Now this is something very different. There are no short cuts here, your book must have its own identity, an identity that tightly hooks into the genre and genre readers. It needs its own website and possibly its own blog. A Book Platform is everything that promotes the book (or a book series).

Now, I understand this may sound a little confusing, but even though an Author Platform and Book Platform are two different things, they do strategically hinge upon one another. So, whatever your book does – launch, be featured in a book club, make the best seller list – will be in both your Book Platform and your Author Platform. HOWEVER, what you do in your Author Platform will not be mentioned in your Book Platform if it does not pertain to that particular book. The Book Platform website will have a media page too, with a press kit that only covers that specific book (or series) and no others.

One more note. If you write in two genres, you will need two book platforms, two separate websites and two different focuses, totally geared toward that genre and those fans. If you write several different kinds of books within one genre – for example, sub-genres of romance – you can get away with one Book Platform, but only as long as you keep each book/series neatly partitioned for its own following. Note: if you write fiction and non-fiction, you will clearly have two different audiences to talk to and smashing them together in one place never bodes well.

The line between Author Platform and Book Platform should not be blurred. For example, if you have created a charity building resource through your non-fiction book about the dangers to wild geese in northern California, you would not discuss it on your Book Website or blog for a book in a different genre. No "save the geese banners" should appear in your werewolf paranormal romance Book Website … unless of course your werewolf saves geese and you can do some genius cross marketing.

It's not impossible to cross-market. I've written an urban fantasy series. I'm also a retired chef, so I'm writing a cookbook series entitled Who Says Vampires Don't Eat? Recipes for the Loving Vampires in Your Life. I plan to do some serious cross marketing. It's not for every variety of genres and non-fiction, but it's something to always keep in mind. Cross marketing is the only time you should see heavy connections between an Author Platform and a Book Platform (or two different Book Platforms). But Cross Marketing is a subject we cover in another part of this book.

Generally, an author who does not keep their Author Platform and Book Platform mutually exclusive is losing the powerful tool of branding themselves, and thus limiting the number of audiences that author will be known by.

A Book Platform should be targeted and clear of any superfluous information that does not serve to promote the book and only the book. Much more on platforms in Part Two, Platform Building.

An easy way to remember how these two platforms work is to imagine who they are communicating with … The Author Platform communicates with the media and information gatherers … The Book Platform communicates with the reader. The Author Platform is your business office … and the Book Platform is your storefront. That said - many readers connect personally with beloved authors, so feel free to add small personal touches to your Author Website.

ASSIGNMENT

I know how you feel. Every author on the planet is so busy the last thing they want to think about is having more work to do. You may be fighting this idea hard, but I would like you to take a few moments and think this through.

Imagine you're in a mall and all you want to purchase is a pair of jeans. Every store in the mall has jeans, but you must search through each one to find the kind of jeans you like. Some stores are mostly men's jeans, others are mostly children's jeans, a few are sultry lingerie type denim stores. Are you frustrated? Yes, you are!

This is what happens when a parent decides to research the author of the YA book her young daughter is crazy about, and she comes across various books on subjects she never wants her child to see. Oops.

Now, imagine you want to see the eye doctor and get a new pair of prescription eyeglasses. But when you arrive, there's a major celebration going on, cake and balloons and confetti everywhere and you know all the employees are drinking that funny purple rum punch. Do you want to have your eyes examined there? Of course not!

This is exactly what happens when a member of the media comes to your Author Website looking for your press release and latest reviews on your recently released YA novel and has to field through all your paranormal romance, erotica, children's and/or mystery book covers, promotions, links and blogs. Your Author Website is your business office. It shouldn't look like a crazy party where all the guests are random and disconnected.

Always give each specific audience what they want, and ONLY what they want. There's no reason why you can't write in a number of different genres, but keep in mind, your YA fans only want to know about your latest YA book, and your Mystery fans don't care that you write YA.

Keep each genre (or genre and subgenre) in a separate book platform website. These are your store fronts.

At the same time, keep your Author Platform website neat, professional, and ready to tell the media what they want to know. It's your office.

Now, if you don't have your platforms separated, start today. Put all those mystery books on one Book Platform website, all your romance and romance subgenres in another Book Platform website, and clean up your Author Platform Website so that it is easily navigated for information gathering.

Oh, and don't forget, with the completion of each element, you have another reason to toot some news on your social media platforms, gaining a renewed interest in your books.

UNDERSTANDING PROFESSIONALS

Now that you've seen all the elements vital to creating your own Book Business Plan, I'd like to pass on some advice and information on all the amazing, ridiculous and important professionals out there ready, willing and able to step in and help make you famous. Use your good common sense and know what they're talking about beneath the big, hard pitch.

Here they come! The Professionals. You know who they are, they're all over the place, in your Google searches, in your email inbox, in the grocery store, your church, writing class and even in your friendships, because someone always knows someone who knows someone who can – you fill in the blank. Some are pounding at you on Twitter either to get your business or tell you how hard their job really is. Some are advertising on your Facebook wall. Some just slip in when you're not looking and some arrive with a fifty piece brass band.

They're recommended by your critique groups, your writing/author groups and often they pop up when you least expect it. (You mean you didn't know that the woman who walks her dog past your house every morning is a marketing expert? The paperboy heard from the neighbor's kid who babysits your niece that you're writing a book and told his auntie, Margie Marketing.) News travels and there are days when these connections seem opportune. At times these professionals seem like gods. At other times, we imagine them to be money-sucking monsters. One thing is sure, there is a need for many of them. The question is: is it your need? Gird your loins, here they come!

- Literary Agents
- Author's Liaisons
- Promotional Agents
- Publicists
- Marketing Experts
- Consultants and Advisers
- Editors
- Published Authors

All experts, all professionals, and all over the place. How can you, the writer just about to be published or the seasoned author coping with these radical changes in the publishing industry, really and truly know who to use, who not to use, who you need and how to control your project through all the craziness ahead? How many of these services are strategic enough to make or break your success? What does your career require, as opposed to another writer with a different book in a different genre? How much can you really do on your own and how do you know if it's time to hire a professional?

Instinct. Sorry, but it's true. Let's take the above list of wonderful professionals and run through their benefits or downfalls.

Literary Agents – If you're seeking traditional publishing you need one, unless you've chosen an independent publisher that does not require representation. You don't hire an agent, you woo them with your query, then they woo you back with their interest and it isn't until they say they'd like the represent you that it's time to take a serious look at their service and success rate. Literary agents are the backbone for the traditional publishing industry as it has been for a very long time, but as you know, the industry is changing and so is this particular part of it. Be sharp, keep an eye out for scams and never pay a literary agent a dime for any service. An agent earns their payment through a percentage of your success – this is why they're so careful about the authors and books they choose to represent. Only with success will they be financially rewarded, thus, only the cream of the crop get represented in the genres or books that particular agent has seen success with. These professionals need to back the right horse. Don't forget – just because you weren't Agent X, Y or Z's right horse doesn't mean you can't be represented by a literary agent. Seeking out, contacting and connecting with the perfect agent for you is a challenge and takes serious, committed effort. Do your homework, be realistic about your work and never give up.

Author Liaison – This is something new and exciting for those seeking self-publishing. These professionals know the self-publishing arena and can connect you with the perfect self-publisher for you and your project. There are things you need to know. Author Liaisons often will charge for services, and in most cases, they will also contract for a percentage of book sales. Below are the Good Hiring Professionals Strategies. This is vital.

Promotional Agents – Do you know what these people are? Often even I'm not sure, this kind of service often smears in with Publicists, Marketing Experts, Consultants and Advisers. You seriously need the Good Hiring Professionals Strategies below to field through this group of pros.

Editors – Don't even think twice, you need editors. Don't wonder, don't look back and don't pinch pennies. Often the editing is part of a publisher's standard service. In the case of self-publishing, a good author's liaison will recommend one or more. Many writers hire editors to do an edit on a manuscript about to go to a literary agent, and all self-published authors must have a full edit or risk looking like a fool.

Published Authors – How wonderful is it when a successful, published author is willing to share his/her trials and tribulations with you? These are the warriors who have conquered the dragons, found their way and continue to venture onto the battlefield! It's not easy to find, you can't just walk up to a successful author and ask for advice but if you find yourself in a situation that smoothes that path, don't be shy. At a writer's conference, sitting at the bar, munching peanuts and Mr. Author is sipping a beer? By all means, smile and talk. Don't bombard him, just be friendly. Another place to learn amazing, valuable information about the process and life of an author is on Twitter, by following author blogs, or friending authors on Facebook. Don't be a nuisance, just absorb. An author won't be charging you for his or her advice, but you do need to take it all with a grain of salt. Be smart about your choices because your time is valuable as well. Follow or chat with authors who write the same genre you're writing and authors who have approached the market with interesting twists or bold strokes. Be inspired or seek someone else.

Now that we've covered the professionals, it's time to talk about how and when to use them.

Good Hiring Strategies

The <u>"Hope is Not a Good Strategy" Strategy</u> – Authors are writers who love writing and in most cases, don't want to do anything but write. Hoping the perfect champion will simply come along and stumble onto your doorstep to whisk you to success is lame and dangerous. If you build your Author and Book Platforms early and reinforce them all along your journey, you have dynamically pushed the tentacles of your project out into the world. Now you have a better shot at grasping the interest of the right professionals. I have a client who caught the eye of an independent publisher simply by chattering on Twitter and having his novel excerpts on his author site. The indie-publisher Googled the author, found his website, liked the concept and, voila. That's not hope, that's action. Strong Author and Book Platforms are the flip side of just wishing victory into being.

The <u>"Just Like Magic Doesn't Mean Real Magic" Strategy</u> – Wow, I've heard a hundred of these stories. Authors have met author liaisons in grocery stores and publicists at the dry cleaners. They've discovered cool promotional avenues over a glass of wine at a club or overheard an editor talking on the train and struck up a conversation. How serendipitous! Or is it? Serendipity is a twist of fate, but is it destiny? I'm not saying that the publicist you met over cocktails is a fraud or incompetent at all, what I'm suggesting is to step back, take a breath and think it through. Too many writers just finish a manuscript and suddenly have a chance meeting with a professional perfectly poised to catapult them to stardom. It could be a golden opportunity or just a red herring. Be a writer. If this plot twist came into your character's life, what would they do? A little research at the least. Take some time and learn all you can about the professional, be sure they're right for you. Ask to talk to their other clients. Have them do a presentation and explain what they can do for you.

The <u>"Comparing Apples to Apples" Strategy</u> – Now that you are finished with your novel or non-fic book, maybe you're ready to hire a professional to help get you to the next level. It may be an editor, it may be a webmaster expert who can assist in building your platforms, it may be a publicist who knows what you should be doing now to assure serious attention later. You might be at the point where you want to hire a consultant to guide you toward which steps to take next. Be sure to look deep when hiring anyone. After all, you don't hire a plumber who arrives without

---

THE PUBLISHER'S PERSPECTIVE

"The first thing I do when I read a query is Google the author to understand the size, scope and construct of their platform, and how active the author is in building that platform. I also search the author's complete bibliography to see what regular readers are saying about the author's work. And I have been known to call a few editors to find out how easy the author is to work with. I will also research competing books, to see how they are performing and how saturated the market is for that topic. If I see that the author has marketability, has demonstrated a sincere interest in building a long, productive career in publishing books, and if the book's topic meets our needs and interests, I'll go ahead and request the manuscript."

~ David Rozansky, Publisher, Flying Pen Press

his tools, or a doctor without a diploma. Your lawyer and dentist have credentials and so should your career professionals. Compare value for your buck, and compare quality based on success rate.

The "Do I Really Need that?" Strategy – Oh the bells and whistles are so exciting! Everything calls to you from fancy-dancy book-videos to mobile apps. Time to be logical. Do you really need it? Does your budget allow for it? And will it advance your visibility or make you look like a goof? Sorry, but I laughed my butt off when I saw an author with a serious novel about addictions had his book cover printed onto a massive coffee mug. On the other side it said, "Coffee, my addiction of choice". I am certainly not saying you should ignore all the bright sparklies out there that might get your book the attention it deserves, I'm just suggesting you think it through first.

The "Down and Dirty" Strategy – Maybe these magical appearances of professionals everywhere hasn't happened to you. So you have to plan, think and choose for yourself if you need a professional and what kind will serve best. Do your homework. Check out websites, compare expertise and price. Know what's out there and understand what kind of professional can truly guide you. There are a lot of cookie-cutter plans and services available, but remember – the industry is changing. You need to determine the kind of professional you need for this shifting landscape. Locate one who moves with the changes and sees these vacillations as opportunities. It's a lucky time. Just because things have been done one way or another way for years does not mean it's the only way to do it from now on. Look for professionals who are willing to break new ground and personalize their service to you and your book.

The "Careful, Careful, Careful" Strategy – It's one thing to look at websites, but another thing altogether to really get a grasp on a professional's skills. These are people. Some of them have amazing websites and work out of their small home office. Some have large staffs and corner offices in high-rise buildings. Is one better than the other? You will need to keep one thing in mind at all times. This process isn't about getting the absolute best of the best, word renowned "name" professional to handle your progress to success. This is about getting the absolute best professional for you. After exploring all the online information you can get, checking them out with the BBB (Better Business Bureau) and asking around about a particular professional, it's time to take the next step. Contact that person and ask for a phone chat. Yes, a phone chat. A conversation where you can hear that person's voice and they can hear yours. A thousand things can be learned by the inflections in their voice, the passion in their words and the questions that they ask. Don't forget to have your questions ready too because this isn't a one-way street, it's a relationship where both parties will benefit. Trust your instincts and know when the discussion is over. Don't get railroaded into agreeing to anything until you've had time to think. And above all, do not ignore your pocketbook. No matter how great a professional and their service sound, if you don't have the budget for it, it's not a good match.

The "Follow Your Gut" Strategy – Okay, you found the perfect pro to get you where you want to go. They have the right attitude and your instincts tell you that you can work well with this person. You like them and they like you. Now, take a day or two, set it all aside and see what happens next. Explore any possible concerns. Is the cost a bit pricey? Perhaps you can negotiate. Is the timing perfect but the market soft for your particular book? Toss it out as a challenge for exploration. Test yourself and the pro to assure everything is up front and clear. Your gut knows more than you think.

Avoiding the "Wannabe" Strategy – Dan Brown's last book was released in the American and the European market at the same time. You want that. Barbara Kingsolver was interviewed in several cities and spoke live in Los Angeles when The Lacuna was released. Oh, you want that too. Charlaine Harris makes appearances at conventions that feature supernatural or paranormal stories in print, television and film. Yes! You want to do that too! An aspiring author you met online has created a dynamic, powerful and exciting website with all the bells and whistles to expose her work-in-progress and oh yes, you want that too. Let's take a moment and look in the mirror. You're not Dan Brown or even the hopeful writer with the fancy website. You are YOU and you can't lose track of it. How and where and when you get your exposure simply can't be based on what another author is doing. Be sure you've outlined your goals and the path to attaining them is purely based on you and your book.

The "Back Up and Punt" Strategy – Everyone has setbacks. Not every professional we think will be perfect for us, is. Sometimes we just have to bite the bullet, say "uncle" and move on. Be careful. As you move along in this visible world, many people will come out of the woodwork to give you advice, free or for a cost, and that advice isn't always necessarily right for you. If a person states that your author's liaison, agent or publicist should have done "this or that" for you, take a moment to think on it. Was "this or that" considered and determined not the correct strategy for your project? Has your pro never suggested "this or that" and why? Ask. You've been working with this pro for a while and should be on the same page, should have gained respect for each other and found a comfort zone for exploring things, even "this or that". If in that exploration it's determined that there's no longer a good match, shake hands, share a hug and move on. Burn no bridges because now you're back where you started and the last thing you need is a reputation for being too difficult to work with. Use a line one might use about an ex-spouse: simply say that the professional was a good publicist (or marketing expert or author's liaison or whatever), just not good for you. This way, no one looks bad. This time you should be armed with even more important questions to ask as you search out a new professional relationship.

The "Track Record" Strategy – This one is just a warning, it should help raise a red flag. Keep a sharp eye on your track record for success with any professional you hire. Set up a monthly telephone conversation to discuss performance (in fact, if your pro is a good one, they may have already begun this practice as a standard performance check with you, the client). This is an honest, up front way of keeping an eye on your path toward success. Things should be moving ahead in increments acceptable to both you and your professional. Another track record to watch is your own. How are you doing with the professionals you're working with? Are you meeting their requests for information or materials on time? Are you compromising their efforts by implementing suggestions some of those unsolicited experts gave you? Are you firing and hiring a new editor or marketing expert again and again? Are you imagining you are the victim? Or can you do what it takes to streamline your focus and truly move toward success. What's your track record?

When and if you decide it's time to hire a professional, which strategy works best? It's all of them - together. When the time is right, remind yourself to seek out and hire professionals who listen to you AND who you are ready and willing to listen to in return.

Part 2

PLATFORMS BUILDING

"You must either conquer and rule, or serve and lose, suffer or triumph, be the anvil or the hammer."

~ Johann Wolfgang von Goethe, 1749 - 1832

AUTHOR PLATFORM AND BOOK PLATFORM. WHAT'S THE DIFFERENCE?

Are you ready to be the hammer and build your future? First let's get a few things clear about Author Platforms and Book Platforms.

I want you to get into a Zen kind of mood. Rather than thinking about building a nice, level platform with heavy slats of wood, nails, a hammer and some paint to make it pretty, let's think of it a little differently. The standard platform is a level, flat, raised area, a dais for standing upon and announcing your intentions if you're a politician. We're not politicians, we're authors and writers and something flat to those of us in the creative state of mind, is simply unacceptable. Our platforms should not – should NEVER – be flat. Our platforms are made up of various levels and multiple points of view, kind of like a stage in a rock concert. We'll have moving parts and raising parts, shifting areas, shiny and subtle surfaces and a whole lot of curtains and smoke and sparks.

If you look at Platform Building as a necessary evil covering the basics for standard exposure, you will not be successful. You'll get some notice and sell a few books, but make a serious mark? Not likely.

As mentioned in Part 1, Creating an Effective Book Business Plan, you do need both an Author Platform and a Book Platform. You need to look at this a little more like a business. Your Author Platform is your business office. It's the place to promote yourself as an author, offer insight to your directions as an author, have a spiffy and updated media room for the media to easily access, and the site should be embedded with an author blog where you regularly communicate with your fans. Sound like a lot? Did you notice what's missing? Your book(s). Yes, of course your books will be listed there but you will not have all the glitz and beauty or fun of your book platform, because the purpose of your author platform is to focus on you, the author.

This isn't a new concept at all. In fact, the smart, big corporations have been doing this for years. For example, Proctor & Gamble has its company website, then each product is listed but has its own website. Why? The woman interested in purchasing Nice & Easy hair color or Cover Girl makeup isn't interested in Old Spice men's cologne or Safeguard deodorant. P&G's home website focuses on their business, their special projects like sustainability, their news and media room and company info, like career opportunities and investments. BUT, all their products are listed with a link to each product's own website.

Slip over to the creative industry and take a look at DreamWorks Animation SKG. The website has everything we talked about as a business site, then pictures of each film which links to websites of their own. King Fu Panda fans get the full panda experience without having to be interrupted by How to Train Your Dragon pitches or Mastermind craziness.

The same with the Mars Candy Company – there's the business site, then all the product sites. I particularly like Snickers, to eat and the site.

These companies do this because it's important to treat each of your audiences in a different way. You keep your business clean and business-like, then have fun with each product site, making it unique and special to the viewer.

Author Platform

You need to do the same, starting with your Author Platform. Here is a list of the basic pages for a simple Author Platform website:

- Introduction/Home: Bio, background, but keep it simple
- Book(s): Again, keep this simple, the cover art, brief 25 word pitch/synopsis and a buy link. Then you link each book to its separate website.
- Activities: It's vital to keep this one updated regularly. This page lists your speaking engagements, release dates, launch events or dates when you'll be interviewed. This page can also include a collection of podcast interviews links or videos of your activities
- Blog: Whatever format you use for your blogging, it can be embedded into your author website, and that blog must be updated regularly. Consistency is the reason people will keep coming back. They'll want to see what's new.
- Media Room: This one is very important. You will include everything the media could want and make it as simple as possible for them to access it. All elements must be downloadable. You also need to put contact information on this page, either your email address or the phone number of the contact who will arrange for further information the media may request. In your media room you need the items listed below. Make sure everything is downloadable, and check that they're working often. There's nothing uglier than a media person complaining that they couldn't download something they wanted. They get irritated and the last thing we want to do is irritate the media.
  - Author photo (current). A professional shot is not necessary but make sure you look professional)

- Author bio, this is a full bio with memberships, awards, association affiliations and special interests. Many interviewers in the media pick up some piece of interest from those kinds of bios and like to use them for casual approaches to the author. e.g. The author lives in her Chicago apartment with her husband, teenage son and three English bulldogs.)
- Image of your book cover(s) (jpg format)
- Brief synopsis of the book(s)
- Copies of all the press releases you've sent out
- All contact information

NOTE: All the items in your media room should also be in your hands as hard copies so that should you come across a contact who doesn't wish to download the items, you can easily snail mail them a packet. A more indepth discussion of how to build your media kit will come later in the book.

Book Platform

Now let's talk about the basis for your Book Platform. This can be a website or blog and it can be as creative as you want it to be. The sky's the limit!

Seriously, the sky's the limit. Convey your book in its clearest sense. Be creative, use color and images. Of course you want the basics.

- Cover art
- Brief synopsis
- Excerpt
- Buy link

After that you can get creative. Do you want to do a special section on each of your main characters? Go with it. Are you interested in exploring the visual angle of the book? If gardening and flowers play a large part in your book, show plants and flowers and talk about them. If your book is about a time in history, maybe you can do a page that features other things happening in that time period, weather events, wars somewhere else in the world, the fashion of the day.

Your Book Platform is the place to show the creativity and strength of your book and your talent.

Now, I know your next question. Do you need a different website or blog for each book? The answer is no, not for each book, but definitely for each genre. Why? As mentioned earlier, it's your job to make each of your fans feel important. If you write both cozy mysteries and paranormal erotic romance, a fan looking for info about your next cozy mystery might feel like they'd mistakenly stepped into a S&M lingerie store if you try to keep those two genres on the same website. Granted, this example is extreme, but I have seen authors try it. They think they're saving time and energy by combining all their books together, but what they're actually doing is alienating fans of one genre or the other.

If you have written several books or more than one series in the same genre, you can beautifully marry them all into one site. But if you have written both fiction and non-fiction, neither book platform will be as effective if you put them together on one website.

Everything about marketing is focused on effectively and efficiently approaching your target reader. Very few readers like both sweet cozy mysteries and paranormal erotic romance.

HOW MUCH WILL THIS COST?

I totally understand. We authors are poor as dirt most of the time and I'm certainly not asking you to get a second or third mortgage just to create Author and Book Platforms. Let's break this down.

<u>Websites</u> – If you can't figure this out yourself, everyone knows someone who can create a website. Ask around. If you still can't afford the webmaster fees, look into simple, DIY, inexpensive formats where you can put together a free website. If even that gets too hard, think about a barter or trade. Someone who does websites just may need some service you can give them. Are they a closet writer needing a reader or critique partner? Would they love someone to do a few errands for them, pick up cleaning or groceries? Help with their files? Can they use a service you're good at, like bookkeeping or cooking? Trade is always a good way to get services you need.

<u>Blogs</u> – Blogs are free. Blogs are easy. Blogs are highly visible and quickly picked up by the search engines. I have seen blogs used as Author Platforms, although they are somewhat limited as far as having the all important Media Room. I've seen blogs used for Book Platform sites very effectively. One thing to remember about either blogs or websites, they must be updated regularly. Pick a schedule and stick to it. You can train your viewer/fans to pop by every single Thursday to see what's happening. But if you skip a Thursday or two, you've lost followers.

ASSIGNMENT

I encourage everyone to search around and take a look at all your favorite authors' online presence. Check out how they're approaching their fans, how they're differentiating their genres, how their communicating with their fans and how they've created their platforms. Some will seem clumped together, some will be smooth and elegant. Some will look expensive, some will look slapped together. Get a feel for book and author platforms out there in your genre. Seriously check out the competition. You and those authors are talking to the same prospective book buyer. How will you communicate with that reader better, brighter, cleaner and with more punch?

A few thoughts on blogging. I understand that busy authors come to the point where they're pretty strapped for blog subject matter. I have seen writers and authors blog on the 10 subjects listed below and strongly suggest you don't make the same choices. At the beginning of each month make a list of appropriate subjects for your four or eight blogs that month, be sure to choose subjects relevant to your author platform and book subject. That way you'll never blog on anything seen here.

TOP 10 LIST OF BANNED BLOGGING SUBJECTS FOR AUTHORS

<u>Recipes</u> - Honestly, unless you have written or are writing a cookbook, don't share recipes on your blog. Viewers aren't interested in grandma's sugar cookies if you write non-fiction

about child abuse, paranormal romance or murder mysteries (to list a few). They're interested in your book subjects, characters and plots. So, unless the recipe directly relates to your book - in this case the recipe is from your murder mystery (minus the poison) - please don't blog recipes.

Family Pictures - You love your children, and what they do is always funny and exciting – for you. Unless you're writing children's books, don't post pictures of your children playing in the snow or on the sand or at the playground or sleeping with the dog. Aside from having nothing to do with your platforms, it's a little dangerous to post pictures of your children on the internet. This is your platform blog and not your personal, private, for-family-only blog, so refrain from sharing kid pictures.

Pets - See point number 2. Same reasons. We love pets, but there's no place for them in your platform blog unless of course your book is about dogs or cats or training them or breeding them or something of that nature. Now, on the other hand, if you can somehow connect animals with your book subject, plot or characters, posting photos of your pet on Facebook or your blog will draw more viewers than normal. Just make sure it's relevant.

Rants - Whatever you're upset about – the cable guy, the neighbor's sprinkler, the mail-carrier, the IRS - refrain from ranting on your platform blog. Especially if you're angry about anyone in the publishing industry. Don't complain about your agent or publisher, don't gripe about other authors, don't say nasty things about an editor. None of that will ever bode well for you, so just don't do it. Besides, no one ever really wants to hear anyone rant.

Complaints - Often I read blog posts which are complaints about blogging. Counterproductive and just plain not smart.

Book Reviews - Don't just randomly do a book review, good bad or indifferent, unless you plan to do book reviews regularly. There's a right way and a wrong way to do a book review and unless you know those rules, you may make a mistake. If you want to make reviewing books a regular part of your blog activity (once every month, for example), by all means do so. Make sure you let everyone know you're doing reviews. But if you just suddenly get an urge to talk about a book you read … go on and mention it but refrain from making it a full blown review. It has nothing to do with your book or your platform. On the flip side, never, ever comment about a review that has appeared about you or your book. It doesn't matter if it's good or bad - you must stay quiet about it. Commenting about good reviews will come across as sucking up and ranting about bad reviews makes you look unprofessional and a sore loser.

Vacations - Vacations are wonderful. Magical. Delightful. But what does this have to do with your platform? Of course, you can mention that you won't be blogging next week because you'll be on vacation in the Bahamas, you may even post a picture of the beautiful scenery when you get back, but please, no big long blog series on the restaurants of Nassau Island – unless, of course your book is about the Bahamas and you are a food critic.

Rejections - Now, I totally understand that rejection is a big part of becoming and being an author. There are rejections from literary agents, from publishers and don't forget those occasional bad reviews. It happens, and mentioning rejections in your blog is acceptable, just please don't become Debbie Downer and make rejection the topic of a huge portion of your blog entries.

What You Are Eating - Are you a foodie? Is your blog a foodie blog targeted to other foodies? No? Then your blog viewers honestly don't care what you ate for lunch. Again, a mention of something you ate that might segue into a subject about writing, being an author, your book or anything generally about your platform works. But to just blog about what you ate for lunch, well, that's simply boring.

Personal Hygiene - No-one wants to know that you're currently prepping for a colonoscopy or how many times you pull a toothbrush across your teeth every morning. No one really wants to know, and that's all I have to say about that.

I should note that all of these topics are taboo in any sort of social media. Whether it's micro-blogging like on Twitter or Facebook or on regular or guest blog posts, these topics should all be banned from your repertoire of things to talk about.

THE DREADED NETWORKING

Brace yourself, it's time to cover social networking.
- Twitter
- Facebook
- Email Lists
- Group Memberships
- Face-to-face Networking
- Your Image
- How all of them are vital to your success

It's a rousing, sometimes heated debate among authors and writers but unfortunately, all that shouting and pouting changes nothing. You must do all of the above social networking for ultimate success. I know, I know, you're a busy person, you don't have time for this silliness, your life is about writing your book and getting it published. Did you know that what happens after that could very likely be drier than the desert if you ignore social networking? If you don't know this fact or choose to ignore it, be sure to pack lots of water, because it will be a long hard trek to real sales success.

The biggest questions and arguments revolve around which social network works best, is easiest, builds faster and gains results. The answer is, none of them. Only creating a solid mix of these networking vehicles (and whichever newer forms of the process come onto the scene) will work. It's like when you have a stain on your favorite white shirt. You start with standard laundry detergent but the stain is still there. Next, you use the pre-treatment and wash the shirt again, still there. Next you add some bleach to the water and try again and voila! Clean shirt. Was it the last process, the combination of all, or the systematic effort that saved your white shirt? Does it matter? Nope. All that matters is that you can wear the shirt again. That the shirt "works" for you now.

The key to effective social marketing is to take advantage of the many and varied audiences, be focused in your follower-gathering process, be consistent and use efficient time management. There are a plethora of books and resources out there on the ever-changing mechanics of each individual social network, so we won't go into those here. You can check out the appendix to find some of my favorite resources. What I want to stress here is that all these tools are valuable, but only if you use them consistently and regularly.

I'm going to keep this information simple and easy to understand. We'll learn how to build each social network, how to use it and how to manage your time with it.

Twitter

Love it or hate it - you need to Tweet.

How to build it – First and most important, make a clear decision as to why you're doing social marketing in the first place. If it's for your personal use, to enjoy friends and family, I strongly encourage you to have a separate account (on Twitter AND Facebook) for personal stuff. Don't mix business with family and personal friends, it never really works for your business. When you have a separate account for your book business that is part of your Book and/or Author Platform, Twitter can be a real boon.

To build your Twitter following, start following people who will read your book, categories that represent people interested in your book's subject, or groups/organizations who could be interesting to follow regarding your book's topic. The best route to take is the "subject hook" route. For example, if you've written a paranormal romance, you want to seek out people interested in anything paranormal. If you've written a mystery, historic, YA or women's fiction, you want to find people interested in those genres.

One way to find them is to use a Twitter client or application - such as TweetDeck. With these applications you can have as many columns feeding the tweets you choose. For example: one column feeding tweets from your already established followers and another column following the word "vampire" or "werewolf" or "witch" if your book is paranormal. In that column, every person tweeting on the subject will appear. Find something interesting? Follow that person and they will very likely follow you right back. I also suggest you have columns following the industry – publishers, literary agents, etc. That way you catch feeds about things you really should be aware of as the industry goes through this big change.

You can also go to the standard Twitter site and look for people under categories. Another cool thing to do is choose one of your followers, check out their followers and if some of those fit the bill, follow them. You can also locate Twitter groups – author groups, writer groups, paranormal, YA, historic or gardening groups (should your book have a "hook" with gardening).

How to use it – Easier than you think, but not at all what you think. Don't get on to Twitter and just blather about anything. No one cares that you just cleaned the toilet, trust me. Make your tweets relevant and if at all possible, value added. One way to do that is if while following the "Publishing" column, if you see a great article on ebook sales or self-publishing revenue or even self-editing, all you need to do is retweet it. That retweet now goes out to all your followers who can benefit from it. If they like it, they retweet to all their followers who in turn may choose to follow you.

You use Twitter to talk about your blog when you've posted a new entry but please, don't just tweet "I posted to my blog" and don't repeat it a hundred times and don't forget to thank the people who retweet your tweet. Courtesy is a big part of Twitter.

When you tweet about, for example, your new blog entry, try to make it interesting. For example, the first time you might tweet "Creativity attacked me this morning" and the link to your blog. The second time (five or so minutes later) you tweet "Are you extremely creative in the morning?" and the link. The third time, "Creativity and Coffee, yum!" and the link. Can you see how this not only makes someone think the blog is worth reading, but also not mind so much that you're tweeting several times because each time it reads different, looks different and attracts different people.

How to manage your time – There seems to be a drama in the people who hate social marketing. I've heard everything from "my time is too valuable to bother with Twitter" to "what on earth would I talk about?" Funny isn't it, an author who can pound out a 90,000 word novel can't find 140 characters to say about it. Sure you can!

Managing your time with social marketing and especially Twitter is about approaching it with a plan. Today your plan might be to interact. In that case you simply look through your feeds, eavesdrop on conversations and just join in. Tomorrow your plan might be to get people to read your new blog entry. The next day your plan might be to play with your book, post the cover art, tease about the plot or mention where you'll be signing books or researching your book. Perhaps the next day your goal is to grow your follower base.

The real key to Twitter time management is so simple you may not even believe it. For example, I get on Twitter for 15-20 minutes, twice each day, once in the morning and once in the late afternoon. My TweetDeck had a column following me and whenever I get on, I respond to people who have talked to me (@rileymagnus) while I wasn't there. I keep my focus for that day extremely clear. So, 30-40 minutes a day, Monday through Friday. No more and no less and guess what? My Twitter followers think I'm there ALL THE TIME. Is this something you want to tell people? I'm so committed to this plan, I actually use a timer, log on and off 20 minutes later, that way I'm not tempted to play too long or get too involved.

ON SOCIAL NETWORKING

A little note on social media sites. They change. They often change very quickly and without warning. New ones pop up every month.

So if there is a suggested procedure in this book for Facebook, Twitter, TweetDeck, LinkedIn, Google+ or the various website and blog services available, it will likely change before the next edition of this book is ready. A crystal ball wouldn't even work in the speedy pace of today's burgeoning technology.

If you come up against a new alteration in how Facebook informs - or does not inform - you of activity, or how your blog suddenly limits or expands tags for SEO, take a deep breath and get creative. Look at it as a plot conundrum and do a little chin boogie to figure out the best way to accomplish a marketing goal under the new and improved (albeit temporary) rules.

Oh, and don't forget to share your findings with your other marketing author friends!

Facebook

Same rules apply here. If you use Facebook for personal activity, you'll need a separate Facebook page or account for your author business.

How to build it – This one's simple. Again, determine who you want as Facebook friends for your book. Obviously people who love your genre and people who are interested in the subject or "hook" for your book.

You can use the Friend Finder, look into targeted groups and even look at your friends list of friends and invite those who are appropriate. If you've opted in for email notifications, every time you invite a friend and they accept you, you receive an email. In that email are six or eight pictures of their friends. Check out each friend and if they fit your criteria, friend them.

Now, one issue I have with Facebook is the occasional paranoid Facebooker, the one who blocks all their personal information. If they've asked me to be their friend, how am I to know if they fit my criteria if everything is hidden? Sometimes I'll check out the friends we have in common. If I see genre lovers like mine, publishers or authors or a specific interest trend I'm looking for, I'll accept their friendship. But seriously, why ask someone to be your friend if you have no intention of being friendly enough to tell me about yourself?

Be friendly, but I caution you not to put too much personal information on your business Facebook. Email is fine, but address and phone number is not necessary. Be careful, but not so careful that you alienate potential allies.

How to use it – Again, it's all about strategy. What's your purpose? Do you want to use your "hook" to get readers interested in buying your book or at least wanting to wait for it until it's available? Then locate that "hook" and use it well. Is your "hook" history? Perhaps you can post one historic fact every day on your wall, something pertaining to your book's plot or character. Is your main character a baker? Post a daily baking tip. Is your "hook" that your story takes place on the Caribbean? Post daily weather reports or photos of Caribbean scenes. Be sure to keep your posts open-ended to invite response. You should also promote your book events and blog entries on your Facebook wall as well as in the News Feed.

How to manage your time – Again, make a plan. I post my "Author Survey Question of the Day" in the morning and just pop my head in every now and then. I love the responses and especially love when the responders begin to chat with each other. My platform is about author success and there's nothing more intriguing than 20-50 authors shaking things up and sharing techniques, ideas and humor about being a writer. I visit my Facebook wall four or five times each day. I don't stay, I don't post more than one question each day plus announcing blog post updates. I don't even go to Facebook on the weekends, and I always find a good time to post my own answer to the question or respond to comments made there.

Email Lists

Did you really think we wouldn't talk about email lists? Of course you need one, a strong, targeted list you build slowly.

How to build it – You can ask people to join your mailing list on Twitter, Facebook, at your websites or blogs. As they join, you compile the special list. This list is for news. Yes, you may also be Tweeting about your news, Facebooking about it and posting it on your Media Room at your website – but a personal-looking email to these people is an added shout-out we all need.

How to use it – Be cautious and never overuse the list. Use it only for big news – getting a request from an agent, signing with that agent, getting a publishing contract, your book's launch date or talking about your big launch party. Granted, you may be far from any of those just now, but you really need to begin building that list today. You'll be amazed how suddenly things happen in this industry and you want to be prepared. Also, remember these are more personal notes, not as straight forward or broad-stroke informative as Twitter or Facebook communications.

How to manage your time – Building your email list is one of those projects that go on in the background. It really doesn't require time scheduling. Just keep your ears and eyes perked for a good person to contact or a good place to invite people to join your mailing list.

Group Memberships

What's your book about? Is there a major gardening theme in it? A medical theme? Legal theme? Coffee or tea lovers theme? Knowing your major "hook" is how you find the right groups to join. Notice I said "hook", not genre. There are easy ways to approach lovers of a specific genre, but knowing your special "hook" and who is attracted to that "hook" helps take you above and beyond the average book promotion strategies. Finding entire groups of people interested in your "hook" makes group memberships a powerful social marketing tool.

How to build it – There are Yahoo groups, LinkedIn groups, Facebook and Twitter Groups under every category you can imagine. Research these groups and if they fit the profile of your story "hook", join. These groups are free, relatively focused most of the time, and packed with interesting people. (Don't forget to join writing groups focused on marketing while you're at it. Every little bit of marketing strategy and success sharing helps.)

How to use it – Let's say your soon-to-be-released book is a sweet mystery about missing cats. You've joined several cat groups, mystery lovers groups and a few book club groups. Now what do you do?

One thing you don't do is start trying to sell them your book. Instead, you simply observe then join in on the conversations about feline behavior or various mystery writers and your favorite books. At the bottom of all your emails will be your tag. In that tag is the only place you mention you have a book coming out. If you've joined and make good friends, they want to know more about your book and where to buy it. If you tell them all that you're doing research for your next book, you'll be amazed how many step up to help you. But, if all you talk about in any group (or in any social networking situation) is your book and when it comes out, all you'll do is alienate the members.

How to manage your time – What I did was join several groups, sit back and watch as the emails came in (I always select the site's daily digest, just to keep things neat in my inbox), and determine which groups had real value for me based on how their subjects and dialogue presents. I finally settled on three groups and simply exited from all the others. If one turns out not to be as good as I thought, I un-join and look for a replacement. I never spend more than a few moments a day looking through the group emails, and I usually contribute at least once a day on a subject that interests me.

Face-to-Face Networking

Remember people? Living, breathing people? The kind you look right at and can touch when you shake hands or give a casual hug? Social networking isn't just internet networking. Granted the internet makes our world wider, we still can't let it limit us in the process. Authors need face-to-face networking too.

How to build it – You have a dentist, a gardener, a vet for your dog. You go to grocery stores and clothing stores and post offices. You see people every single day. Open your mouth and talk. When someone on the plane asks what you do, tell them you're a writer. Tell them about your book(s). When the eye doctor asks what's new, tell them about your coming book release. SPEAK and be heard.

How to use it – You can't always be talking about your book, but you sure can get the message out to people not on the internet. If your book is being released, make up a flyer, copy it and post it at the vet's, the dentist office, the grocery store, even in the library. Find authors in your neighborhood or community and join forces to do live book events. Become a social butterfly and take the moment to really shine where people can see you doing it. As I said, the internet is great, but it's not everything. Besides, fresh air is good for you. As a published author, one of the most important things you can do is to carry a copy of your book with you at all times. Keep one in your bag, a few in your car and some in your day-job office. If you're only e-published, keep your Kindle or your smart phone loaded with your book(s) at all times. When you mention what you do, it's very powerful to be able to show people what you did.

<u>**How to manage your time**</u> – Schedule everything because every moment you're doing your face-to-face reach, you're not at your keyboard. Work smart and strategically. Keep those flyers in your car so that you can take one with you every time you run an errand. Trust me, the perfect bulletin board is waiting for it.

The Perfect Mix

All of these elements of social marketing are extremely important, but the perfect mix is a recipe only you can devise for yourself. It will depend on your genre, your time and your energy. It will be affected by your deadlines and real life obligations. The main goal here is to manage to do a little of every one of these networks, find the right combination of time and effort and let it become second nature. Once you're active with all of them, only one thing can happen – you become visible to the world and that's a good thing!

Your Image

My pet peeve! Read this section very carefully.

You are a writer. You are an author. You are a professional! So please don't post a picture of your dog or cat as your avatar for Twitter or Facebook. Don't show me a photo of you wearing a Halloween costume (unless it's Halloween) or drinking from a two-canned beer helmet at the ballgame. I don't want to see a picture of your kids. Don't show yourself as a couch potato or a general slob in an oversized sweatshirt with an unsavory statement plastered across your chest. I don't want to see authors wearing bikinis or sunning on the beach. At the same time, I don't need to see them working hard at the com-

I DON'T WANT TO!

All you writers out there, I know you. I'm one of you. I'd rather be sitting at the keyboard in my fuzzy bunny slippers and track pants and writing feverishly than deal with the scary world out there. Most writers are shy, bashful and a bit withdrawn. It comes from spending most of our time inside our wonderful imaginations. Unfortunately, we all have to come out of the turtle shell eventually to market ourselves and assure that the book we toiled over will be successful.

K.M. Weiland, author of Behold the Dawn, was asked how she overcame her introverted personality to so successfully promote herself and her books.

"Sheer willpower! I would much rather turn off the internet and hibernate with my latest work-in-progress, I had to make a choice between what was most comfortable (not marketing) and what needed to be done in order to move forward with my writing career. One of the key realizations for me was that I could go as slowly or as quickly as I needed to. I didn't need to jump in right away with a 50-city book tour. I could start with easy things, such as a blog and a Facebook account. The good news is that the more you promote yourself and your books, the easier it gets to move past your insecurities."

puter either. There has to be a middle ground, right? It's your avatar … it's how we think of you.

Remember, some publisher or literary agent is scanning your Facebook or Twitter account. Readers are viewing these images. A little dignity goes a long way. You don't need an expensive professional photo of yourself making you look like an IBM employee, but a nice photo wearing neat clothes works real well. It could be taken by a friend, shot outside or inside, smiling or not. Whatever works for you and your personality. If you're a wild one, show it with a twinkle in your eye and what you say in your social networking, not by making a radical fashion statement.

Using your book cover is good too. If you don't have a book cover yet, you can choose an image that represents your book. But I will advise one thing strongly. Don't change your avatar too often. It makes it hard to recognize you. That avatar becomes the image we look for when we're following you, so change it no more than once or twice each year.

ASSIGNMENT

Try creating a daily list to keep on schedule, do all of your social marketing AND make sure you don't spend too much of your valuable time doing it. Try to keep your total social networking time to one hour each day, 5 days each week. Take Saturday and Sunday off and use those days to focus on your writing plans for the next week, have dinner with the family or maybe a few glasses of wine with friends. Balance is the name of the game.

Social Networking Daily Checklist

TWITTER

Image acceptable?	Yes
9:10 AM – 9:20 AM	Done, logged off at 9:20 AM
Social Tweets	4
Promo Tweets	4
Retweets	3
Followers Growth	Followed 3 from Urban Fantasy book clubs
4:40 PM – 4:50 PM	Done, logged off at 4:51
Social Tweets	6
Promo Tweets	2
Retweets	4
Followers Growth	Followed 4 from last week's #FF
Total Time Spent	21 minutes

FACEBOOK

Image Acceptable?	Yes
Initial Post of the Day	Done
Social FB	Responded to 2 posts in the News Feed
Promo Posts	1 promoting new blog entry, posted same at 8 FB groups
Friends Growth	Accepted 2 new friends and requested friendship of 2 new Urban Fantasy Book Clubs
Initial Post response	Comments and "Liked" comments posted on original post
Total Time Spent	15 minutes

EMAIL LISTS

Added to Fan List	4, as requested through book website and blogs
Added to Media Contact	6 - 4 local media contacts and 2 updated contacts
Added to General List	6, new friends met at ballgame, interested in book news
Total Time Spent	10 minutes

GROUP MEMBERSHIPS

Search New	Joined 2 FB Urban Fantasy lovers groups and joined 1 new Fiction Readers Fan group on LinkedIn
Responses to existing	Looked through daily digest emails from my LinkedIn and Yahoo groups, chose to exit from two and responded to one
Total Time Spent	10 minutes

FACE TO FACE NETWROKING

#1	Talked about book at the dentis'st during checkup, posted flyer for the book in employee lounge
#2	Chatted about book while helping at son's school lunch
#3	Talked about book with waitress who mentioned she loves vampires
Total Time Spent	5 extra minutes beyond normal time spent

TOTAL TIME SPENT ON ALL SOCIAL NETWORKING 61 minutes

KNOW YOUR MARKET

I cover this in almost every workshop I teach or speaking engagement I do and we covered it briefly under the Book Business Plan section. Here we're going a lot deeper, because knowing your market seriously impacts the power and effectiveness of your platforms. Who are you writing for? What are they looking for? How can you expand your market by playing the "Genre Game"?

Earlier I asked you to do a little research, discover how many books are out there in your genre and who the top sellers in that genre are. I wanted you to visualize the vastness of this playing field in order to grasp the importance of understanding your market. Most authors don't clearly understand the market much less their market. Now that you've done that research and have a clear idea, we're going to cover a deeper way of analyzing that market and using what we learn to give us a leg up against the competition.

Most times in the past, a reader/book buyer would determine that they liked a specific genre – romance, adventure, historic, literary – then go searching for books in that category. It was fairly easy for readers to find those books because publishers went to a lot of effort to promote new books and authors. These days it's different. Authors don't have publishers covering the marketing and exposure responsibilities any longer. In the olden days, promotions went out, speaking and book signing schedules were set, even travel fees were paid by the publishers. Not any more. In fact, with most publishers (even the big ones) unless you're an A-list author, the most you can expect is a listing in their catalogue. Times have changed, big time.

This shifting paradigm in the publishing industry isn't over yet either. When it's all done the industry will look very, very different. I'm no analyst and I can't see the future, but I do see one thing. Our careers are in our own hands now. An author can look at this as a disaster or as a fantastic opportunity. I say opportunity! I say let's see how we can make it great.

Who are you writing for?

There's a benefit to going rogue – or in this case, picking up the ball the publishing industry has relinquished and running with it. This is our opportunity to shine and show that we can do it better than they can anyway. Almost every month we hear a story about a self published author selling an amazing number of their books and the big publishing houses knocking on their door. If they can do it, so can you and it doesn't take away your fortune or all your writing time. It will take some time for your first book, but as you all learn when checking out Author and Book Websites, once an author passes a certain level of fan harvest, less work is required. Their fans become another powerful marketing tool because their fans are so plenty, they can be heard chattering about the book all over the world. It's a noble goal, to build such a reader base. It fills the coffers and smoothes the path for future books. So, who are those fans? Who are you writing for?

You should know everything about them, from what other genres they may like to read, their station in life and their preferences in other entertainment. How old are they? Are they primarily female? Male? How are they reading books? In front of a fire on weekends with a glass of fine brandy? On the train with their Kindles? At the library? In school?

One way you can learn all this is to take a look at successful author blogs in your genre category. Read all the responses. Another way is to go to Amazon and read the reviews of books in your genre. Envision these fans. There's a lot you can glean from the type of writing, the user name they use and how they use vernacular. Are they your fans too? Should they be? Without knowing who your fans are or will be, your marketing is sort of directionless, like shooting fish in a pond or using a shotgun with hopes of hitting a singular, defined target. You have to know who you're marketing to, otherwise you're spinning your wheels.

What are they looking for?

Now that you've defined your fan or future fan, determine what they're looking for. Are they adventurous people who absolutely love being surprised? Are they sweet romance lovers who will not tolerate an author rocking the boat? Are they young adults who seek the dark stories or young adults who seek the bright, entertaining stories? Do they have a strong sense of morality? You need to know what your prospective fan is looking for in the books they read or you could lose them, no matter how hard it was to gain them.

It's a respect game. They expect you to continue to deliver and by respecting that, you get to continue serving that fan base. Note: some authors get bored, this is why they write in several genres and to several different fan bases. It's not necessary to use a different pen name, but it is important to have separate Book Platforms to target and serve each of these audiences.

Expand Your Market by Playing the "Genre Game"

Now we're going to have some fun. I'm going to start off with a story I heard that basically opened my mind to creating this element in the platforms workshop.

Once upon a time – only a few years ago – an author by the name of Danielle Trussoni (a woman who had written a non-fiction prior, a memoir entitled Falling Through the Earth), wrote a novel entitled Angelology. Her agent pitched the book again and again as a literary piece of work with nothing but negative results. Then the agent got creative. S/he began playing the "Genre Game". Looking at the manuscript, s/he listed the elements – angels, religion, adventure, danger, a race of half-angel/half-humans (Nephillim) that threaten human existence, a magnificent, beautiful male Nephillim-villain, budding romance and redemption. Which way should the agent go? I'm not sure of the process used, but when Trussoni's agent went back to publishers, this time calling Angelology a supernatural horror, the book no one wanted suddenly spurred a bidding war; and rumor has it, the author received a massive advance. Her second book in the series, Angelopolis, is in the works.

This story may be true or not but when I heard it, it made perfect sense to me. Everything about a book is intimately connecting with how that book will be marketed. Without possible or probable profit, there's no point in the big publishers taking the financial risk of publishing. This makes me believe that at least the core of this story is absolutely true.

Now, what happened with Angelology might happen all the time. I'm not a literary agent and like all industry pros, I'm sure they have their secret tricks up their sleeves. I will say one thing about this situation, it opened my mind to some fantastic possibilities for authors.

Did you know that when a book is pigeon-holed as a particular genre it is primarily for ease of categorization? It's not always right or complete, but if a book is called Urban Fantasy, it has certain elements that will easily fit onto a "shelf" making it easy for readers and book-buyers to find. That's what genres are actually for, sales targeting.

But think about this. Even though Amazon or B&N or your literary agent or publisher are calling your book Urban Fantasy, what else could it be? List all the elements. Does it have paranormal romance elements? Are there hints of horror? Humor? How about specifics? Does the book have zombies or vampires or werewolves or all of the above? Does it have a unique twist making it political or does it deal with racial issues?

Now take a look at the lists you made earlier about your reader, what they like and what they're looking for. Yes, your book may be categorized as an Urban Fantasy, but if you target possible buyers of Paranormal Romance, they might love your book. If you locate groups of zombie, vampire, or werewolf lovers, again you might have expanded your fanbase. If your book is categorized YA, remember, more adult women read YA than young adults. Does your book explore religion? Should you approach spiritual or Christian groups for book exposure?

The key to playing the genre game isn't to deny the primary genre of your book by style or story, it's to expand the exposure of your book beyond the bookshelf category mentality. It's about getting more sales.

WARNING! There are things to watch out for. Know these genres very well. For example, if you've written a Murder Mystery, tread carefully in the Cozy Mystery genre. Those readers generally don't like colorful language or sexual themes. If you've written an Urban Fantasy that has sex elements but no love, approach Paranormal Romance readers carefully. If your manuscript only briefly explores an historic era, don't try to sell it to hardcore Historic Fiction fans. As mentioned earlier, respect the reader. It will always pay off.

These are not new, crazy ideas for promoting and marketing your book. This style of expanded marketing has been around since long before Barnum & Bailey raised their first big top in 1881. Attracting as many readers to your book as possible from as many angles as possible is the key to real sales success.

ASSIGNMENT

Okay, so for your assignment let's REALLY play the Genre Game! Take a stack of 3" x 5" white index cards, a red Sharpie and a blue Sharpie and clear off a table so that you have a lot of space to play on.

With the red Sharpie, write one of the primary genres on each card.

- *Romance*
- *Mystery*
- *Military*
- *Women's Fiction*
- *Historical*
- *Fantasy*
- *Horror*
- *Western*
- *Time Travel*
- *YA*
- *Children's*
- *Steampunk*
- *Science Fiction*
- *Spiritual*
- *Memoir*
- *Non-Fiction*

- *Literary*

No, technically memoir, non-fiction and literary are not genres, but to play the Genre Game effectively and find new audiences, we're going to add them in.

Now, use the blue sharpie and write one subgenre on each card.

- *Paranormal*
- *Urban*
- *Mystery*
- *Horror*
- *Supernatural*
- *Steampunk*
- *Authorian*
- *Comic*
- *Dark*
- *Mythology*
- *Heroic*
- *Contemporary*
- *Erotic*
- *Gothic*
- *Futuristic*
- *Historical*
- *Time Travel*
- *Western*
- *Romantic*
- *Spiritual*
- *Post Apocalyptic*
- *Military*

You will notice that several of the genres will also appear in the subgenre cards, no worries, this will also help locate new readers for your book.

Now, turn over the genre cards and mark the back of each one with a big red "G", and turn over the subgenre cards and mark the back if each one with a blue "SG".

Lay out the cards, face down on the table and just start playing. Pick one "G" card and one "SG" card. If neither work for your book, do it again, and again and again. During this process, your mind will begin to take a few new concepts into consideration. For example, could what you thought was merely a Historical Romance also possibly have enough subgenre horror or military or mystery or comic or supernatural elements in the manuscript to attract readers of those kinds of books? Consider each possibility as you go through the cards. Stack the good possibilities aside for further exploration and continue until you've gone through everything.

The point of this assignment is to a) get you to have some fun playing the Genre Game and b) open your mind to some possibilities you hadn't thought about before. The more plausible genre and subgenre mixes you can find for your book, the more target audiences you have for your marketing!

EFFECTIVE PRE-LAUNCH PLANNING

Many times I've met an author who's totally excited that their book is coming out soon. They've told their friends about it and even signed up for speaking engagements and a virtual blog tour to help promote the book. Then they discover the launch wasn't everything they hoped. They did everything right, so what went wrong? Simple. They didn't push further, stretch the envelope or expanded beyond the standard tried-and-true formulas. These days it takes more than average approaches to the market to make serious sales, especially if you're a first-time author, or perhaps just launching your second or third book.

I once met an author whose book was coming onto the market in three short weeks, and she'd been incorrectly told not to promote it until it was out and available.

Don't mean to sound brazen or mean but ... shizbutt-hog-wash-are-you-crazy-you-cannot-be-freaking-serious!

Okay, now I feel better. You see, there's a certain madness that overcomes authors when they get close to seeing their book in the flesh that makes them forget all the good sense that got them to that point in the first place. I call it The Dreaded Almost Famous Syndrome. It causes all kinds of crazy things to mix and mash in your head until it's a pulverized tomato soup, you know the kind I mean, right out of the can and tasting like nothing, not even tomatoes.

But never fear, there is a cure for The Dreaded Almost Famous Syndrome and it's far simpler than you think. Ready?

Common Sense

I told you it was simple. See, as the circus rings tighten around you and everything in the big top is bright and shiny and distracting, there's a simple way to extract yourself from those terrible "squirrel" moments and keep on track. Just use your head. All the experts in the world and all your friends and all those strangers who come out of the woodwork to give you advice (some out of caring, some out of jealousy, some for money) are going to start sounding like an off-key brass band tuning up. If you use your head and categorize all the ideas that are being lobbed your way, you will see things clearly. You are smart. And you are definitely smart enough to instinctively know when a piece of advice seems wrong.

That author I mentioned earlier with the book about to be launched? After we chatted she said the words I knew were coming. "Oh my God, I thought that might be wrong! It didn't seem to make sense, I just didn't know what else to do but follow the plan and wait until after the book came out. Now what do I do?"

I told her not to panic, and suggested that from that day forward to always remember: No matter what, if it doesn't smell like apple pie and it doesn't look like apple pie, it probably isn't apple pie. In other words, she needed to trust her instincts and promote her book.

A successful pre-launch campaign for any book hinges tightly to your platforms. How and where are you visible? How many audiences do you speak to? Are they targeted book buyers? If it's your mom and that nice kid at the Home Depot, you don't have a platform, or an audience for that matter. If you've built your platform carefully and developed a visibility, your audience – all those followers who never miss your blog, chime in on Twitter, support you at the critique groups and email you to be on your mailing lists – has been there through it all. They've watched your initial struggles with writing or rewriting or editing your book. They've stood and cheered when you got an agent or found a publisher perfect for your book. They've listened to you talk about the book cover and shouted rousing congratulations when you finally showed them how it looks. They pop in at your book website often to see what's new and get the skinny on your progress. And if you've done all this well, that group of followers has grown and grown.

Timing is Everything

T Minus 90 Days (3 Weeks for E-Pub)

Now, time for the countdown. Three months before your book comes out (if hard published, three weeks before if e-published) you begin your serious hype. Using every venue you've cultivated with your social and personal networking, you announce when the book will be available. You begin promoting pre-sales of the book. You send out your first well crafted press release, making sure to target local papers and publications, radio and television stations. You make sure you've gone the extra mile by sending that same press release to your friends, family and associates. Arrange a book Launch Party with a local independent bookstore or library and begin compiling an invitation list. Be sure to include other authors, friends, family members, business associates and local media (newspaper, television and radio) on that list.

Any book is worthy of a celebration book launch party - epublished or paper published. You can do it in person, set up your laptop and let your guests purchase your book online. You can do it in chat format making sure everyone gets the buy link for the book. And by the way, a few e-publishers and app builders have even developed a way to sign ebooks! Cool, huh. So no discounting some of these pre-launch elements just because you're only e-published. Remember, soon everyone will be e-published.

And no matter how you're published, regarding the planning for your launch party, don't forget your unique "hooks". Theme the party with them and expand the invitation list to include them.

GETTING REVIEWED

First time author? Maybe this is your tenth or twentieth release. Either way there is nothing more important or effective than gaining reviews for your book. You need to start early and continue well after the book is out. So, where do you find people to review your book? Finding reviewers is as easy as finding a roofer. Just Google book reviewers. Keep an eye on the Facebook and Twitter feeds and make sure to click that link every time one of your author friends posts an announcement that their book has been reviewed. Is that a good reviewer for your book? Does that book review blog have a good, target and strong following? Check the comments at the end of a few of the other reviews. Were there several, or was there just one or two? Have you checked into your genre target for reviewers? For example, if you write about vampires, there are easily a hundred blogs, review groups, paranormal book lover groups and independent reviewers available for the picking. Now, all you need to do is take the well crafted 25 word pitch, write a review request and bam, you get reviewed. Never underestimate the power of a good review. If a review blog has hundreds or even thousands of subscribers and they decide that they love your book, you can gain some terrific sales. More established authors can take advantage of not only these online blog reviewer opportunities, but with their already rocking platforms, they can send requests to major newspapers as well.

T Minus 60 Days (2 Weeks for E-pub)

Two months before the launch, (2 weeks for the e-pub crowd) you strike again, but make sure your message is bigger, denser and more powerful. Now you take any early copies of the book and seek reviews. Getting those advanced reader copies to book bloggers and reviewers is key to hitting the ground running. You begin booking yourself to speak and have events at libraries, coffee shops, bookstores and book clubs, to be interviewed with online groups and guest blog. Another press release, this time attaching your photo, the book cover and announcing the venues where the book will be available and where it is already available for preorder. Traditional and e-published authors, remember that nifty Media Room you created for your Book and Author Websites, this is where it really comes in handy. Remember, the press is online as much as print these days so there's lots to say and a ton of venues to be sending press releases to.

T Minus 30 Days (1 Week for E-pub)

Books in hands from the publisher? Get them out and visible. Carry them to the local independent bookstores and libraries and show them off. Arrange for book events. Keep your ears perked for major book events you may want to participate in.

E-pubbed authors, this is where your social networking starts to shine. It's a week before your book is available. Start contests on Twitter, create a buzz on groups and take advantage of virtual book tours. Always keep searching for more directions and avenues for finding even more possible book buyers.

T Minus 20 Days (5 Days for E-pub)

Get your Launch Party invitations out. Send out another press release about the Launch Party. Respond immediately to RSVPs. Hopefully you've already begun speaking at groups and libraries or online and by this point, have most likely been interviewed for a few radio shows or online shows. You've been invited to guest blog and have hyped the coming launch on your book website, your own blog, Twitter, Facebook and every email group and subject interest group pertaining to your plot "hook" you belong too.

T Minus 10 Days (3 Days for E-pub)

Now you can hear harmonizing circus music, but don't let it distract you. You're very close, be sure to keep the momentum up. Continue to book speaking arrangements, even if they're at a local high school writing class. Continue to Twitter and facbook, blog, guest blog and email. Get really excited! You need to be as visible as your book. Continue to let everyone know where they can preorder a "signed" copy of your book, and keep telling everyone the launch date.

Launch Day

Send a press release announcing everything important, that the book launches that day, where it can be purchased, where you have been interviewed and the great reviews you've gotten. Get over to your blog (there's time before the party, honest) and give your followers your heartfelt thanks for taking the journey with you. Get to your book website and splash that banner that the book is now available! Keep your site media room up to date and loaded with activity so everyone knows where they can see you or hear you speak.

Now, go to your party, have a glass or three of wine, enjoy the crowd and pat yourself on the back for making the day what it should be. Doing an effective pre-launch you've accomplished several things.

- You've pre-sold books
- You've targeted book buyers interested in your subject "hook"

- You've become visible and created a demand for your book
- You've made yourself media available and created a fan following
- You've eliminated the stress of worrying about failure because you've done your part to assure success.

Now, of course, every book and every pre-launch will be different. Some topics may easily lend themselves to exciting, highly visible exposure. Others may take a bit more push. The level of push is all on your shoulders though. It's your choice. You're the author and that is your baby. It's up to you.

ASSIGNMENT

The first thing your must determine is what kind of a book launch you want. Something old-school and traditional with book store book signings and speaking engagements at book club meetings? Or perhaps you want something more techie, internet and real life interactive and sparked with all the special things technology can do. Before you plan anything, make a clear outline of the kind of book launch you want.

Remember, if this is your second book and you didn't do it this way last time, it doesn't mean you can't or shouldn't try this technique this time. Nothing sells a first book more than a major splash for a second book. Another thing to consider, are you print and ebook published, or just ebook published? This will make a clear difference in your timetable, as you saw in the basic traditional vs. ebook launch scheduling.

Now, for your assignment, take a calendar and some plain paper and start. As suggested earlier, start from the end – your actual launch date – and work backwards. Schedule in your teasers, social marketing, budget and press releases then get very tight with your plan.

For example, if you have a press release scheduled to be released on June 4 announcing the release of the book, make sure you have a small check list under that notation. Something like this.

- *Press Release finished*
- *Press Release list completed*
- *Online Press Release Distribution Service chosen*
- *Budget $?0*
- *In the same vein, if you have another planned notation that on July 16 you'll be sending out a press release announcing the book launch party, now that little check list will be a bit longer.*
- *Press Release finished*
- *Press Release List updated and complete*
- *Online Press Release Distribution Service tested and chosen*
- *Location for party secured*
- *Invitations prepared*
- *Invitation List complete*
- *Invitations sent out by _____*
- *Refreshments contracted and clean up crew arranged*
- *All follow-up calls to confirm arrangements made on _____*
- *Budget $X.00*

So, as you can see, it's one thing to plan your launch and have a pre-launch schedule of events, but every item on that list requires a little more. Making lists like this help to cover contingencies that might arise. For example, if you call early enough to confirm the caterer and discover that they lost your order and can not fill it, you'll have time to make other arrangements. If you're on top of everything, you can recover from ANYTHING.

Create an imaginary pre-launch campaign now with all the elements and secondary elements you can think of, this way you'll be ready for the real thing when the time comes and you'll become very savvy at planning, something you'll be doing a lot of as your marketing adventure continues.

"Action is the foundational key to all success."

~ Pablo Piccasso, 1881 - 1973

TIME IS ON YOUR SIDE

I understand it's scary, especially if you're further along with your platform and promotional plans and need to catch up with a well rounded, powerful platform strategy for both your book and yourself as an author. But trust me, time is on your side.

At this point I want to say that I've heard it all – every excuse, every complaint, every indignity about how authors are supposed to be authors and nothing else. I can only assume that everyone reading this book knows that the times, they are a'changin'. The key to true author success is to know what you're up against and know that you are in this for the money.

Face it, writing has become a performance art and if you want to be an author, you have to do the job of getting the message out. Samuel Clemens knew it, and now so do you.

Time is on your side, honest. Whether you're just starting this journey, well into it and looking for more effective ways to get exposure, or discovering that this industry is nothing like you thought it was, time is on your side.

You just can't waste it. If an author tells me they can't find time to build platforms and don't believe in wasting time with social networking and refuse to compromise their art by becoming sales people, I usually have only one impression. They don't want it bad enough. But you do. You're not about to waste your time looking for reasons not to build your own success.

KEEP IT ALIVE

Your platforms should be living, breathing, growing things and only by keeping your ear to the ground and your eyes wide open will you be able to shift and adjust to the changing industry. There's an opportunity, an idea seed, a new "hook" angle or a great concept out there at any given moment. You just need to look for it. That's the only real way to keep your platforms, fan base and future book sales alive and well.

Knowing where to look for new ideas isn't all that hard. In fact, all it requires is to open your eyes. Get your nose away from authors and books and look around at this big, loud world. You can't walk a block without being exposed to some kind of marketing for some kind of product.

Was there a really amazing slogan on that exterminator van that just drove past? Is it the kind of approach you could use for your next book? Did you see a gorgeous CD cover for a band you never heard of? Is that the kind of image that could work for your book cover or avatar? Did you see a fabulous website but it was for a bakery or law firm or jewelry manufacturer? Study the website. What attracted you, what held your interest? The colors? The navigation? The images or message?

The ways to keep your platform alive are everywhere – on the radio, in television shows or ads, in the striking ad you noticed in a magazine. They're on billboards and in the middle of a song you just heard.

I encourage you all to keep a file of these ideas. That slogan, picture, tidbit of lyrics, even the unrelated website can be the seeds to something you never thought about for promoting or marketing your book. If there's a promotional event that impressed you, make note of it. Some version of that, shred of it, or energy from it just may give you a new audience or approach for your books. You can use paper or go electronic by using some sort of note-taking app like Evernote - either way works. Platforms and marketing strategies are happening all around you all the time. Just because it's a pharmacy commercial doesn't mean there's not some fiber of brilliance in there you hadn't thought about before.

We've all heard it a thousand times! To write well one must read well. To create beautiful art, one must look at beautiful art. Well then, to develop fantastic promotions and marketing campaigns, one must observe fantastic promotions and marketing campaigns. Lift your eyes and observe.

Keeping your platforms alive means breathing along with all the other platforms in the world, not just the publishing world. Some of my best ideas came from completely unrelated promotions. They inspired me, made me think and being problem solvers, thinking authors can create amazing success.

TIMING AND IMAGE

Timing and image work hand in hand. Ten years ago, the image for e-publishing was non-existent. Now it's front and center. Could there be a better time? I think not. With traditional publishing practices shifting like the San Andreas Fault, there was only one way for e-pub to go, to the front of the class. There was a time when self-published authors were not respected, now traditionally published successful authors are choosing to self-publish. And when a new author self-publishes and does their selling job well, traditional publishers are scrambling to sign them up.

The image of everything in the publishing industry is changing in everyone's eyes. Don't get me wrong, bad is bad and a bad book, no matter how it's published, will always be bad. We're not worried about the writer without the brains to take a few writing classes or hire an editor. We're not concerned about the author who writes down their thoughts for fun. We're interested in the author who wants success.

The timing and image of your exposure should ride smoothly along with the industry. It's one of the main reasons I suggest that you follow publishing professionals in your Twitter feed or on Facebook. You can't be successful if you don't know what's going on in the industry. There is a lot of press on predictions of the state of books in the next 5-10 years. Keep your finger on that pulse.

Another rumor that directly affects all authors of fiction and non-fiction is that within as few as five years libraries will be going cyber. It will save money in purchasing books, heating and air conditioning books, paying staff to handle the books and tracking down book thieves. Many authors count heavily on library book sales. How will they adjust and alter their approaches to the market now? With fantastic creativity, that's how.

It's a brave new world. The fact that you're preparing your platforms says we'll all be here and thriving for a long time – as long as we adjust and grow and keep our platforms energetic and relevant!

ASSIGNMENT

Choose your favorite author and follow them on Twitter, friend them on Facebook, get onto their blog email feed and start analyzing. What are they doing that interests you? What are they doing that no one else is doing? What do you like and not like about their platforms and social marketing? What would you do different? Now do the same with your favorite band. Then do it with your favorite restaurant or online magazine or newspaper. After jotting down all your impressions, take a long look and you will discover not only a common thread, but the undeniable uniqueness of every approach.

Part 3

TANTRIC PUBLICITY

"What kills the skunk is the publicity it gives itself."

~ Abraham Lincoln

DEFINING PUBLICITY

Is there anything sexier than the media? Glitz and glamour, fantastic events that blow the mind and make Average Joe a household name? This section of this book is designed to teach the practical side of publicity, familiarize you with the rules of the game as well as a few of the tricks for getting major results on a shoe string budget.

Position 1. Samprayogika – The Embrace – Defining Publicity

This is the foreplay part of publicity, it's where the author starts to understand, attract and hold the attention of the media. We'll talk about relationship building, targets exploration, and uniqueness of approach.

Welcome, welcome one and all! This is the fantastic, amazing and exciting world of Publicity for Authors … that sexy, shiny and remarkable tool that when used correctly, can take you from unknown author to … the sky's the limit!

Did that feel a little like a carnival barker? That's kind of the old-style view of publicity but this chapter is designed to help you see the sensual, subtle and quiet power of publicity that works to underpin the strength of your campaigns.

There's a distinct difference between other forms of product exposure and publicity. We're going to explore the essence of this tool as well as how to create relationships that will make things much easier down the road when you really need it. Call it foreplay, call it the embrace, call it IMPORTANT because it is.

Publicity has been an enigma to most authors. Let's start by helping you identify publicity in the world around you.

PUBLICITY: an act or device designed to attract public interest; specifically: information with news value issued as a means of gaining public attention or support

PUBLICIST: one that publicizes; to bring to the attention of the public

Who can afford a publicist? Not most authors I know, so we're moving ahead with all the basics needed to create the sexiest publicity possible for you and your book.

Familiarize yourself with what publicity is, and what is not. For example, an advertisement or announcement about a promotion for a product in your local paper is not publicity. A news story in your local paper about that product, who invented it or distributes it is publicity. The perfect storm is when the ad for that product and a positive story for that product appear in the same issue. Score!

Know why you need publicity. You need publicity to put yourself and your book in front of prospective readers and book buyers; to be recognized because you used as much creativity to publicize yourself and your book as you used to write it; and to get results without having to rob a bank.

Understand how publicity happens. Sometimes publicity comes with something remarkably good, sometimes just the opposite. The key to managing this powerful tool well is to control how publicity happens and be prepared when it happens without your intent. One thing you must realize though, without publicity, very little can happen to advance your cause – the exposure of your book.

Understand how publicity works. Think "network". Think "community". Think "connection". Until not so long ago, the way publicity worked was simple – it focused on exposing and making a product desirable. Today, a broader brush paints that approach and includes working though various connections, communities and networks to massively expand your exposure.

Know how many levels of publicity exist. Above I mentioned three of the seven levels of publicity – network, community and connection. These seven powerful levels of publicity can be easily developed to expand exposure. These will be covered in the next section

Know exactly what you want. Like tantric sex, good publicity requires a clear idea of your goals. Reaching climax in the form of massive books sales is of course the answer, but how do you define your publicity climax? For example, if your book is a mystery, you may want to play your publicity plan just as carefully as your story plot, with a strategic feeding of information designed to build to a crescendo at the moment of the book's release. You may choose to do teasers to pull prospective buyers on board. You'll need a plan for all of this, a strategy that plays with your communities, networks and connections, but also feeds the media information the way they require it. A good lover knows when and how to hold back or press the envelope, but more important than that, the lover knows clearly which lover s/he can and which lover s/he can not do what with. Know your goals and understand the playing field.

A publicity story may be quietly pushing a book, fashion, social issue or coming event for a cause, but in all cases, you'll need to look carefully to see how the publicity is orchestrated for its strongest effect. It may be using a person's celebrity to push a cause to the forefront, but in equal return, expand that celebrity's exposure. It may be that a person or company simply wants to align themselves with something to help their own cause.

Example: Author James Doe spearheads a foundation to support the protection of east coast dunes. Dunes all along the east coast of America are melting away and taking with them hundreds of species of insects, turtles and … (you get my drift, some paragraphs down you will probably see something like) … Mr. Doe is donating a percentage of profits from his newest book entitled 'Castle of the Dune', a futuristic fantasy, published by ABC Publishers and available this month. For more information about Mr. Doe's 'Save the Dunes Foundation', please contact …

ASSIGNMENT

Peruse the newspaper (in hand or on line), take in the television and radio news and check out everything you can in community communications – i.e. business or community newsletters, neighborhood tabloids, church bulletins, etc. Find all forms of pure publicity and make note of them. Think about sexy approaches, about subtle approaches and carefully look for what the piece of publicity is trying to expose (promote or sell).

THE MEDIA KIT

Position 2. Arts, Knowledge & Chemistry – The First Touch

Now that you've explored the media landscape for publicity samples, what did you think of what you saw? Did you find items that you suspect may be very successful? Did you see a few that looked like they couldn't help but fail? Did you see some things that made you wonder if the media was being manipulated? Did you see a few that made you laugh, wondering who'd really believe that James Doe's "Save the Dunes Foundation" was anything more than a ploy to get more people to buy his book? Or, did you find yourself believing that he loved and cared deeply about protecting the dunes?

Perception is everything. In planning a sexy publicity campaign for you and your book, you probably can already see that careful groundwork needs to be laid. If your book is a memoir about your crazy childhood growing up in an ashram, you probably wouldn't want to connect your book with the Beef Council of America. It might be a more thoughtful and productive alliance if you choose to support the Organic Food Growers of America.

Not that every publicity plan needs to include the alliance with some group or organization, but it doesn't hurt. Connection is the primary objective of the Seven Levels of Publicity, so don't discount it.

Before we discuss those Seven Levels of Publicity, let's cover a bit about structure. Do you know what should be in your media kit? The Media Room is the most important element of your Author Platform website. In order to truly understand how to make your publicity most effective, you'll need to know and implement the elements necessary. I'd like to expound a little further than I did earlier in the Platforms section of this book.

A Powerful/Sexy Media Kit

The Perfect 25-30 Word Sound Bite. This is your elevator pitch on steroids. It's primed and sexy and powerful and proud as possible. It explains what your book is about, what you are about, who will buy your book, where they'll buy it, and how you plan to expose it. This, and your 10 word sound-bite, will carry you from query to live broadcast interviews, it'll be the identifying mark within all your platform elements and be a showcase in most of your press releases.

Bio and Photo. Your bio must be true, accurate and impressive. It should identify you as the one and only person qualified to write the book you wrote. Your photo must be up to date and attractive. Yes, I know you prefer to sit at your keyboard wearing a stained tee shirt and baseball cap but trust me, you are not making the kind of statement you want to make by using such a photo in your Media Kit - or on your Twitter or Facebook page. Do yourself a favor and be honest with your photo. Remember who is looking at it – i.e. television and publication people who might want to interview you or include your photo in their story. Remember the movie A League of Their Own? No one wants to be the Marla Hooch who only gets the long distance shots or radio interviews. No, we don't all look like a super-model, but respect yourself and what you've accomplished. Do your hair, put on makeup, wear a nice shirt - get someone to take a flattering picture of you. Use photo editing software to get rid of that scratch your cat gave you last night. But that's it. Be proud - you're an author.

Book reviews. Yes, you want reviews, even if your book is not yet published or still in the publishing process. Get professional friends to review your book. Other authors who have been published are a great place to start. Ask a college professor. Invite someone who is an expert on the subject of your book to give you a review. The more sterling the source, the more likely the review will stick, and who knows, possibly become part of your future press campaign or a quote on your book jacket cover. Newer, more influential reviewers and reviews will eventually begin to replace these original ones (or not, if you've really kicked butt and gotten good ones). Never forget all those reviews you get on Amazon. Learn from them, use them and make sure people know about them.

Excerpt Chapters. There are conflicting views on offering sample chapters to the public or media but I am of a strong belief that if you grab the attention of a reader with enough to hold their interest, and in an environment where they feel privileged to get the sneak peek, then you've sold a book or gained a fan, or better yet, an interview with someone in the media. Whether self published, e-published, indie-published or mainstream published, I strongly suggest that an author retains promotional and publicity control of their story. You should be able to offer between one and five chapters of your novel to a promotional or publicity audience. You should be able to read a full chapter at a book event. You should be able to promote and approach the media with any elements of your book.

Media Room. This is a vital component of your Author Platform. It is a page on your website (or blog or Facebook dedicated media page, etc.) totally dedicated to your publicity and media exposure. On that page you will have announcements of your upcoming book events, where you'll be speaking or doing a reading, what events you'll be attending (conferences, writers groups, library events, etc.) who will interview you and who has interviewed you. You'll have links to your book video if you have one. Links to your online interviews, links to video interviews, podcasts and links to all places that your book can be purchased. In your media room you will also keep a running update of your press releases, the most current at the top.

A Plan. This is the most important element of your media kit because it states clearly that you're not going to simply disappear, that you have writing projects in the works, future books for a series or additional interests that will lead to books.

Think of your Media Kit as the place for the reporter to find everything they need to confirm that yes, they would love a one-on-one interview with you. If they don't choose to interview you (as some media outlets are smaller and not staffed for interviews), they at least have the information you most want them to know at their fingertips so that they can download and use it in a story. This kit should be designed as a mini-catalog or magazine format which can be printed, emailed or downloaded as a pdf. The elements within the kit (photos, schedules, etc), can also be available as separate downloads. Make sure your downloads are in a non-editable format such as pdf and jpg and not as word processing or other editable documents. Check every item often to make sure the downloads are working.

Now, let's talk about all the ways to connect and spread out.

The Seven Levels of Publicity Connection

Local. Never discount your local venues. Make flyers and post them at the grocery stores, in your dentist, vet or beauty parlor waiting areas. Let your local papers know that a local kid did good and got a book published. That's at least one sure way to get not only a small story to plug into your Media Room, but perhaps even a review or two.

Community. What do you belong to in your neighborhood, city or state? Are you on the board of directors for anything? Do you participate in neighborhood food or clothing drives? City marathons? Work at state election polls? If not, step away from the keyboard, put on a pair of shoes and get out of the house. Get involved with communities that relate to your book subject. Non-fiction writers will find this easy, but fiction writers get a little confused. Never fear, it really is easy. Is there a bakery in your book? Perhaps it's the location of a key plot event? Maybe one of the main characters is a baker. Get involved with bakery associations. Offer to write for their newsletters, help organize events, anything that gets you closer to people who might really enjoy buying and reading your book. Using community can be tricky though. Obviously you can't join today and start spouting off that your book is for sale tomorrow. Just like online involvement, take your time, make friends and when you know the time is right, toot your horn. Community, by its nature, supports its members. Two or more communities make that support even stronger.

Network. Still we haven't left your home town, but now we're diving deeper into not only your book for clues about where to network, but we're seeking more professional connections. Now's the time to make really good friends with your city or state-wide libraries, radio station personalities, newspaper reporters, television reporters, chain and independent book store owners/managers. You will be giving a few books away to this group. Your goal is to make them aware that you've written a book about to come out, that you are willing to talk about it, and that you are looking for reviews. Bribery helps, but only when appropriate. For example, the bakery plot point mentioned above? Take a pie or cookies when talking with these media people. Also, don't originally seek them where they work or at their office, try to cross paths with them where they live. If the local rhythm and blues DJ shops at the same grocery store you do, be prepared with a sample book in your bag when you go shopping. Don't be obtrusive or obnoxious, but do remember that people generally like people, and a person who works in the media, is always looking for interesting people to interview or talk with. Networks grow from such encounters. Mr. R&B DJ might not be able to talk about your Bakery Mystery book, but he knows someone who knows someone else. This is how a serious networks starts. Besides cookies, remember to repay a favor whenever you can. It keeps your network alive and well.

Memberships. What organizations do you belong to? Can those organizations benefit and be a benefit to you in connection with your book? If you're an artist and you belong to a graphic artist's organization (local or national) and perhaps one of your characters is also a graphic designer, maybe you're in the right place to do a little horn tooting. If not, seek out organizations that will logically work. It shouldn't be very hard, you did write a book about this or that, so it must already interest you, right? Memberships serve several publicity needs – they provide another exposure to prospective book buyers, and they look very good on your bio too.

Expertise. What do you know? If you're a foodie and there's a foodie in your book, now you're an expert at all things foodie. Create a blog, invite other foodies, offer to guest blog on other foodie or restaurant related blogs. Always tag your guest blogs (that tag, by the way, will not be about your book, but about your foodie expertise) with a small mention at the end linking to your own foodie blog, your book's website, your author website and your book's purchase link. It's like an afterthought that tells the reader of that guest blog that you're not only a great foodie who writes a great blog entry, but a great writer who wrote a book they'll be interested in. Keep that information unobtrusive, in small type, but like a little tag that packs a major punch, because now you've gained a fan through the blog you just wrote on Polentas of Southern California. See, easy. You're already an expert at something that relates to your book.

Online. As stated before, you must Twitter. You must Facebook. You must blog. You must be involved with other bloggers and guest blog as much as possible. You need to join groups that focus on subjects in your book. You need LinkedIn. And you have no choice if you want to be as highly visible as possible. Oh, and yes, you need to start now if you're not already doing this. Why? Let's say you're looking for an agent or publisher. They will do a Google search and if they find only a few listings, it's very likely you're going to be low on their interest list. If you have several pages listed under your name, their interest is raised, clearly observing that you are an author looking for every opportunity to advance your career and sales. Do you think for one moment the media isn't thinking the same thing? If a reporter Googles you and sees mad activity, that's where their news nose will go. A vibrant, active and exciting online presence is your foreplay with the media.

Media. Always start locally, as the "home town hero" approach is always a good bet for first exposure. Create a list of local radio and television stations. Look into all the local newspapers and magazines. Search each of their websites to locate the perfect contact. Next, look into online media, radio shows and video podcasting networks. Moving still deeper, look into state-wide and national media lists that can be purchased. If budget allows (and we'll talk about that in the next section) and the list serves your needs, make the purchase. Now look into online press release distribution services. Learn everything you can about these services. Who uses the AP Wire? Who offers international press release distribution? What do you really need and how does each service fit into your plan.

One more note: naturally under this category we are discussing the media, but I want you to also remember that word-of-mouth is the biggest publicity exposure out there. So, when you do begin sending out press releases, don't forget to send them off to your friends and associates. Even if Uncle Fred hates Paranormal Romance, he may proudly tell someone at work that his niece has just gotten one published and that associate may buy the book. Discount no one in your publicity efforts.

ASSIGNMENT

Take some time to look carefully at the Seven Levels of Publicity Connection, then create a list exclusively for you and your book

1. *Local*
2. *Community*
3. *Network*
4. *Memberships*
5. *Expertise*
6. *Online*
7. *Media*

Under each of these Seven Levels of Publicity Connection, list how you are already active, how you plan to become active, and how you plan to implement your strategies.

Do you already talk around your LOCAL neighborhood about your life as an author, your book and your future? Are you even seen in your local venues? At the cleaners, grocery store, vet? Some authors hardly ever get out of the house. Put on some shoes and take an umbrella.

How do you plan to get involved with your COMMUNITY? Can you volunteer for food drives or neighborhood cleanup projects? People love being social while doing these kinds of things, and you might make a few friends as well as book sales.

Are you NETWORKING? Looking for those special connections?

Do you seek meaningful and related organization MEMBERSHIPS to be active within? Are you shouting your EXPERTISE, doing it ONLINE and off line and most of all, are you making friends with the MEDIA?

Start today and make a plan for using all seven levels. Complete the list and keep it posted near your computer. You never know when a new venue, group, organization or activity might pop up that seems perfect for your strategies. Keep adding to your Seven Levels of Publicity Connection lists and one day it'll be second nature and you won't even know you're doing it!

PRESS MANAGEMENT

Position 3. Practical Climax – Well Planned Press Exposure

Press exposure is kind of like leaving your curtains wide open. Passersby can look in or not. What will they see? Is the living room clean and neat? Did you leave a racy book on the coffee table? Is the dog sleeping on the couch? What are you telling the viewer about who you are and the way you live? If you know that one of the folks passing by was a newspaper journalist who likes to look for the "dirt" on people, would you be more careful about leaving the curtains open, or would you be more careful about what he could see through that window?

An author who assumes becoming successful is all about their books and nothing else is not seeing the whole picture.

This is how it all works. You, the author, have an image you want to portray. It may be that you're a little crazy like your book's plot and characters, so your attire is always a little odd, interesting and fun. It could be that your book is a non-fiction about how to be flawlessly organized, so your chosen image is that of a flawlessly organized person. Maybe you write deep psychological novels and your image is that of someone cool, calm and collected like your heroes or heroines. Either way, the first element of a well planned press exposure is to determine what image you want to portray.

This isn't about making something up or playing pretend. It's about actually being who you are, only making sure who you are is digestible for the public. By manipulating the media, many authors have pulled off the unthinkable – written memoirs full of lies and been busted for it, or written beautiful novels based on the high visibility of their celebrity or nobility only to be dropped hard when the truth of their personal character was brought into question. Facts are facts and the media's job is to dig the truth out of your publicity. Unfortunately, the press isn't interested in "innocent until proven guilty". The press will assume the worst and grab a shovel, especially if you become very popular very quickly. There are ways to control this kind of thing.

Always be truthful. Always tell the truth in your press releases, your bios and even your photos. If they sniff one lie, they'll dive in for the others, and there are always others. We learned that when we were what, five years old? One lie needs another to cover it, then another and another. It's the fact about dishonesty that never changes.

Control the flow of information. You can control how you feed information through carefully designed press releases that tell only what you want about you and your book. This is the "crescendo" plan that flights press releases out in even bits until the full exposure is revealed. Some call them teasers.

Respect the Media. If you want respect, you need to show it first. Never mass email press releases. Carefully choose the press contact you want to cultivate. Never harass the press for results and by all means, never ever send releases that are not news. Empty press releases – ones that repeat the same information as your last press release – are a sure way to get the wrong reputation among media reporters.

Never jump the gun. Don't push out information before it is really information. A press release announcing that you may be doing a book promotion at the same location and the same date as George Clooney is doing a book signing, is jumping the gun. Two issues with this. 1) The press doesn't care about what "might" happen, only about what "will" happen. And 2) if your book has nothing to do with George Clooney or his book, what's the point of mentioning it? Jumping the gun with badly thought-out press releases is another way to make enemies in the media.

Be fair with the press. If you are the kind of author who only leaves the house for cigarettes and book signing events, it's cool to admit that. Saying that you're always bopping around town doing this and that or supporting one cause or another when it's not the truth (or not currently the truth) is not being fair. What will you say when a reporter asks, "What charities are you supporting?" Answering "Um, I'm thinking about supporting the local Animal Rescue League" just won't cut it. You weren't fair, didn't actually tell the truth and just wasted that reporter's time. Do you really expect to see him at your door again?

Well planned press exposure starts with identifying what image you have, deciding how or if you want to polish it, and showing it correctly to the press. Don't open those curtains until you've done these things. Your book may be spectacular, but if the press proves you to be a liar on any level, they'll tell the public you're a liar and the public is less likely to purchase the book written by a branded liar.

Powerful Press Management

Press management is based on a well thought-out timeline and information flow. A typical press campaign plan will be developed from the end forward, for example, the planning starts at the major point of exposure – for example, your launch date. For the sake of this exercise, let's say your book will be released on November 2. Now, work backwards.

Obviously your book launch date will be the key piece of news, but what else prior to that is news? Determine those points and fill out a press campaign that covers three months, ending with your big date on the timeline.

The final Press Campaign plan might look like this:

- Release dated August 3, announcement that Denver resident, author Mary Smith, has been signed by ABC publishing Company for her first novel.
- Release dated August 17, announcing that the author has launched a Media Room on the book's website, making available all announcements and press kit materials for media convenience.
- Release dated September 7, author announces that she will be speaking at XYZ Writing Conference on the subject of "A First Time Author's Journey".
- Release dated September 21, author announces that ABC Publishing Company plans to release the book on November 2.
- Release dated October 5, author announces that she will be interviewed on "Book Talks" radio show by Jane Doe on October 10.
- Release dated October 12, announcing plans for a Book Launch Party and the cities scheduled for a book tour to begin November 14.
- Release dated October 26, announcing the details of the November 2 Book Launch Party, where it will be and that the media is invited to enjoy refreshments and talk with the author.
- Release dated November 3, announcing the success of the launch party, who attended, comments about the book and where the next book event will be held.

All those "events" above – the XYZ Writing Conference speaking engagement, the radio interview, the book tour and launch party – yes, you must create those opportunities yourself. Make the contacts and get on the schedule. That's how you'll have news to tell the media. Also, keeping your press campaign plan flexible is vital, you never know what might come up that qualifies as news. Listed here are the basics, but if you receive an honor for some other short story in the meantime, that can be made into news. You'll want to announce every interview you give, and you may want to let the press know if a notable book reviewer has given you a great review.

The key here is to not overwhelm the media with press releases. Don't be a yippy dog. Combine information when appropriate and seriously consider if a piece of information is truly newsworthy. If you've made a friend in the media, a reporter who often responds to your releases, make closer friends, don't be afraid to call that reporter and ask if a bit of information is news or not. They'll help.

E-Published?

The Press Campaign will look different, and be even more effective!

It's a fact, e-pubbed books are geared to screen readers who are wired for the internet world of communication. If you are a smart publicist for your book, e-pubbed or not, you understand that the internet is where the real action is happening in real time.

Using the same timeline (only it will be a bit tighter as e-publishing can happen much quicker) e-pub authors will still create press releases informing of the same important events. Online publicity must be even more flexible, because everything moves faster in the cyber world.

Note: As we all know, all books will be e-published, so the landscape is vacillating in a good way. Avenues are opening daily in preparation of this coming event, and it is very important for current e-pubbed authors to keep their ears perked and eyes open for growing publicity opportunities. The trick here is to take advantage of what you have (an ebook) where it is most purchased and read (the e-readers available and internet) for the biggest exposure bang. Let's look at the press campaign again, this time as an ebook moving around the e-world.

Your press campaign will cover probably six weeks and not three months.

Your announcements will be similar, but who you announce to will be slightly different. For example, instead of announcing to *The New York Times* print book editor, you'll be announcing to *The New York Times* online book review editor and the ebook reviews editor. You'll also have a plethora of additional venues to make your announcements. In your blog, on Twitter, Facebook, LinkedIn, at online groups (especially groups with interests that might be similar to your book – a book with a divorced woman finding her way might be a great read to members of divorced women online groups), and any online group designed to help authors promote.

You, more than traditionally published authors, will want to consider a book video, as people who prefer ebooks love anything technical and available on their screen. Announcing the launch of a book video is news.

You need to seek speaking opportunities – perhaps you can do a Q&A on a Facebook writers group. Maybe you can be a guest speaker during an online chat regarding your particular genre. If you can't find such opportunities, make them. Offer them to the groups you already belong to or groups you'd like to be associated with. All this is news.

Seek out reviews. All authors, e-published or traditionally published, need reviews. Online reviews can be wonderful. They have the same immediacy that selling an ebook on line has. Good reviews are newsworthy.

Can't do a real world book tour because there is no hard book? Two suggestions. 1) Do the cyber book tours, they're easy, fun and active. All you do is an interview with the blog owner. Reach out to blogs by other writers and authors, but also be sure to reach out to blogs that touch the subject "hook" of your book. Check out the subject related Yahoo groups and ask them to be part of your blog book tour. A blog book tour is news, especially to the cyber loving universe. 2) No print book? Consider POD. Talk to your publisher, or if you're self published, look into the POD option for your book. These print-on-demand books are sold on Amazon and everywhere else your ebook can be sold. Purchasing a small quantity of these POD books can allow you to have a physical book launch tour at small indie bookstores who may want to sell your ebook and POD books on their websites, or libraries which are always happy to get people in the door for events. If you bring your own books, you can do a book signing event anywhere, in a park, a coffee shop, a bakery, anywhere that is connected to your book subject, "hook" or genre.

You want a launch party? So, have one! You can party hardy online. Create a Yahoo group or message board for your book and let the fun be had. Invite everyone in to chat and enjoy themselves. Blast it to your online media contacts, through your blog, online groups, Twitter, Facebook, etc.

The primary goal of any Press and Exposure Campaign is to let the public know you have a book for sell – and to get sales.

Press Release Format

We briefly covered this earlier in the Creating an Effective Book Business Plan. A press release is usually less than 250 words and it answers the following questions:

- Who
- What
- Where
- Why
- When

No more and no less. Common elements in every press release must include the following:

- A contact name and email and/or phone number
- A powerful, but CLEAR headline (don't be cryptic)
- The basic information including book title, author name, author website address, link to the website Media Room page, and where the book can be purchased
- Your 25 Word Pitch
- The news you want to release.

ASSIGNMENT

Make a list of all the possible press releases you could send out for your book. These press releases can cover everything from signing the publishing contract to the actual launch date. You should have between five and ten press releases BUT WARNING! Each press release MUST BE NEWS!

What is news? Not the second of what might be ten versions of your book cover. Not retelling everything about your publisher's contract with only one change, something about a new publisher's assistant working with you. Imagine yourself as a newspaper reporter. Do you want to take the same old story your editor let you run two months ago – again – and try to convince him that this new "assistant" is a development worth wasting space on? Or would you rather take something totally new and exciting, like the fact that you are supporting a major charity with the sales of the book, or that your launch date is set and a party planned at a beautiful old library slated to close soon. Think NEWS when writing your press releases. The point of sending them out is not just the activity of doing so, it's the life blood line of news. Never abuse it. If you have no news, you have no press release.

Get creative and make your list. The NEWS ideas may be possible or seem outrageous right now, but get the nuts in the grinder and build a press management plan. You might be surprised how many "nutty" ideas turn out to be real news story makers.

The process is simple – make the list, hone the list, make the plan and implement the plan.

FOLLOW UP

Position 4. Post Success Bliss - Follow-up Strategies.

Keep the love alive. After your first book publicity and media campaign, you want to make sure all the media friends you made, remain your friends. Don't be afraid to drop them a line, a simple thank-you for covering your launch event, or printing a brief story about your book. Say thank-you for helping you get a review, or recommending another venue, newspaper, magazine, radio station or interviewer to you. This way when your next book comes out, they're more likely to remember your courtesy and respond again.

Also, in an effort to follow up on your press campaign, should something wonderful come out of all this – a movie deal, the sale of European publishing rights, or some astounding high sales volume – you can and should ship out another press release to let the world know. News is news!

The media contacts you make and connect with are no different from your professional or personal relationships. They ask for honesty and clarity but on a deeper level, they are asking for a little more.

If a media contact has been great to you, keep in touch. Of course, you're not going to be popping an email over to their office twice a day, but a monthly note wouldn't hurt. I'm not talking about a media contact who reprinted your press release once over the course of your campaign, I'm talking about that one reporter who showed up at your events, made suggestions to help you with your contact list, wrote a great story and/or did a great interview. That guy should know you not only appreciate him, but like him. He's the one who wants to know if your next book is on the way, what it'll be about, and how he can help you again. This fellow might not work for the biggest, brightest newspaper, radio or television station or magazine you contacted. In fact, he may just be a young go-getter working for the smallest news outlet in your town but young budding journalists who have go-getter genes never, ever stay put. This dude is a contact now and down the road. Who knows, before your next book comes out, he may be working for *The New York Times*. This guy is going to remember your respect and especially your appreciation. If he's not the go-to contact at *The New York Times* and you still keep in touch with him, he will find the perfect contact for you. That's how making media friends and keeping them works. Don't forget anyone as you climb your ladder to the top.

At the same time, when cub reporter nice guy leaves the local paper for *The New York Times*, don't forget the paper he left. Small town or not, they would like to be on top of your media list, after all, they're the ones who supported you with your first book. When your buddy tells you he's leaving, have him introduce you to his replacement. Be nice, make friends and make note of the new reporter's name for your constantly updated media contact list.

Everyone counts and every media outlet is vital. If you eventually choose to hire a press release distribution service (you can find them on line and use them easily for distribution of your press releases), whether for national or international contacts or to reach the AP wire, never, ever forget your local small guys. Many city papers and media contacts are never reached with those large lists (lists that you really never know the contacts for, since all you are purchasing is the distribution service). You never want to lose your connection with the original and local town, city, state or territory contacts you've made.

Be diligent on keeping your contact lists current. If you are unsure of a contact, if they had moved on or been promoted, check. Take pride in your publicity contacts as well as your publicity plan.

Refresh and Refresh Often

There's always something new. Keep your ears perked for the new fangled media option, whatever it is, whatever form it takes or where ever it comes from. There was a time when the only way the news was spread was by mouth; then newspapers; then telegraph; then telephone; then internet then … we'll see! How exciting the world is and how fast it grows. Don't be left behind. If you catch something on Twitter that seems ridiculous, something so far fetched it seems impossible as a publicity exposure option, watch it carefully. You never know what wonderful things are being developed to help get the word out. The future is always sneaking up and surprising us. Use those surprises to your advantage.

The Unspoken Agreement

I'd like to offer a final few words about the media, the public, your peers and your fans – there's an unspoken agreement you must adhere to where good publicity is concerned. It's a promise to be honest and tell the truth. To be the best author and human being you can be. To hurt no one – not exactly the Hippocratic Oath but it means the same – don't damage someone else's career for the sake of your own.

Now granted, most people are willing to be this way, but few understand the power of this unspoken agreement. Break it once and you can almost kiss your career goodbye. Sure, some come back from breaking this unspoken agreement, but it's never the same for them or their fans. Think Richard Nixon. Think Pete Rose. Public Relations Damage Control is a nasty, nasty place, almost like the waiting room in the movie "Beetlejuice".

Part 4
GEISHA MARKETING

"An ounce of performance is worth a pound of promise."
~ Mae West, 1892-1980

GEISHA TRAINING

Geisha Marketing is specifically designed and presented to show the true art of marketing, to imbue the power of passion, skill, creativity, understanding and talent to create a successful book marketing plan.

> MARKETING: The process by which one creates customer interest in products or services.

> GEISHA: An entertainer whose skills include performing various arts such as classical music and dance.

The best way to begin is to explain what Marketing is NOT. The biggest confusion comes with the obvious. Marketing is not promotions. It is not publicity. It is not research and it is not about numbers. It's ALL OF THOSE THINGS but in its own beautifully wrapped package. We're going to explore how marketing works for your particular author needs.

Particular needs? I understand why you're asking. Too many people think marketing for authors is regular old marketing and if you just pick up a Marketing for Dummies book you'll have it made. Wrong. Marketing for authors has a very specific challenge. For example, are you traditionally published with good distribution? There's one way to market for that. Are you indie-published with a less wide distribution? A different marketing strategy is needed. Are you self-published with limited or no distribution? This requires yet another marketing strategy. Are you e-published or POD published? Yes, you get it – there are as many different ways to market books as there are ways to publish them.

A Geisha is an entertainer who knows her audience, understands their interest level and performs her art for the highest response. The trick to doing this for your book is to know the tools and use them elegantly.

Geisha Tools

A Geisha has her makeup, her kimono, her fan and her musical instrument. She honors those tools by keeping them neat, polished and organized. That way, when she needs them they're perfect and ready. An author's tools are a little different but just as vital.

The Author's Makeup – Your makeup is your image. You've created it and perfected it. You already have the photo of yourself representing the image you want to convey, and created the perfect, polished and honest bio. You've placed these things neatly in your Author Website Media Room and should the media come to take a look, they'll be impressed with your professionalism.

The Author's Kimono – What have you wrapped your image in? I'm not talking clothing here, although you should be sure to appear presentable every time you speak, do a reading or simply attend a meeting or event. When I ask what you've wrapped your image in, I'm asking what have you done to create an aura of information about yourself, information you control and feed to the world at your discretion? Have you chosen your information and venues carefully? Twitter? Facebook? Well developed email lists? Group memberships? Who surrounds you and how does it shed the right light on you and your work? If you write about vampires and are a member of every goth group on the internet, that's the image you want and have planned. But if your book is about raising children, and your personal interest is in goth related things, you may want to rethink how to present your image. Perhaps use a different username for the vampire playtime and your real name or pen name for your author image. Image and perception is everything when marketing yourself and your book, and if you haven't prepared and polished it yet, you need you get yourself wrapped in the correct kimono to move ahead with your performance.

The Author's Fan – Now let's talk about how you dispense information. Under that last point I mentioned Twitter, Facebook, emails – just about all forms of electronic social marketing – that's part of an author's fan. But remember, the whole world is not electronic. The majority of books are published electronically, but people? People are not and never will be wholly electronic oriented. We still go to the grocery store for milk, go to see the dentist or doctor or lawyer, get on a bus or in our cars to go to work. In other words, even if your book is e-published, don't forget that people exist in the real world. Of course, it always plays best to promote ebooks inside the box (the computer) because a majority of ebook readers are most often on their computer, but they're also eating at restaurants, shopping in shoe stores and watching television. The use of an Author's Fan is to fan your marketing wide. Don't flitter small puffs of possible sales your way, swish that fan for the broadest exposure. If all you do to market your ebook is talk to computer users, you've missed a major opportunity to not only market to those same people in several ways and places, but to get to those magic three exposures that finally make a buyer buy. If you're traditionally print published, do the same thing, get your exposures in different venues besides print venues. Reach the internet crowd as well as people where they actually live and breath in their real lives. Wave that fan as far as your arms can reach!

The Author's Musical Instrument – How powerful is the harmony of your marketing?

The musical instrument must be tuned and shiny clean. All of your marketing, no matter how you're published, must sing with perfect timing and elegant melodies. Never try to market a book that can't be bought anywhere yet. Instead, establish a crescendo buildup with beautiful teasers, joint exposure with like or similar events or elements that compliment your book. If you've written a book that has a strong gardening element, perhaps a romance that takes place in a beautiful park and one of the main characters is an expert with roses, find your crescendo with gardening groups and clubs, guest blog for gardening interest groups and join the local or national gardener's society. Create harmony with readers of interest in your book's subject matter.

Geisha Goals

Do you know your goals? Have you seriously thought about exactly what kind of success you want from your book? So many writers and authors tell me, "I so hope for a top ten best seller!" Well, unfortunately I'm here to tell you that hope is not a plan. It's not a strategy and it sure isn't a goal. If you want to sell 1,000 books within a month, you're halfway there. A strong, committed goal spurs all kinds of creativity. A Geisha's goals were to please, and yours must be pretty much the same. You need to please your prospective readers and you must make sure your marketing plan feeds into your sales goals. If a possible buyer of your book doesn't know about it, never hears about it, has no clue what it's about and never heard of the author, well your goals are most likely going to fall very short. Goals generate plans, plans generate activity and activity creates visibility which leads right back to those goals being met.

Creating Perfection – Perfection is what's perfect for you. If your book is clear in your head (that means, you can tell someone in 25 words or less exactly what your book is about), if you know who your prospective readers are and if you understand the responsibility for real success is yours and yours alone, perfection will also become very clear to you. Like the ideal background music in a dramatic movie scene, everything is going to come together. But none of that will happen without all the other elements. Your tools and sharp goals will help you create perfection exactly as it should be, for you and your book.

Polished Speaking, Appearance and Pride – Authors will always find themselves in a situation where they are asked to say something about their book. It could be anything from a family get-together to an invitation to speak with your writing groups, "like interest" groups, or at a conference of some sort. Among the most important elements for this Geisha Performance are the following:

Speaking – Do you know what you're saying? Can you clearly get your message across? What do you sound like when you speak to a group? Take a tape recorder and listen afterwards. Do you say "um" or "like" too often? Is your voice too soft and quiet or too loud? Do you talk too fast or too slow? The only way to know is to listen and analyze yourself. A geisha learned early exactly how to give her listeners what they were looking for. If they required a little humor and laughter, she understood how to do that. If they wanted chaste quiet and the perfect facial expression as the geisha spoke, she did that. Every time you speak to a group you need to take a moment to observe and determine who those listeners are and what they're looking for. Never compromise your personality. This isn't about changing who you are, it's all about polishing it and making it palatable to your audience. Know your listener and you'll have all of their attention.

Appearance – Some authors believe that being the scruffy bohemian is the only way they're willing to appear. Uncompromising attitudes like that are limiting and with the dire need for authors to market themselves, that particular luxury is long gone. If the author is speaking to a group of scruffy bohemians, fine, wear the ratty old inside-out sweatshirt and flip-flops. But, if the audience is a little more neat and proper, clean up your act. The trick here is to find the perfect medium to keep you comfortable and not make a possible buyer of your book uncomfortable. If you are appearing on television, ask the producer or interviewer how you should dress. If you'll be interviewed on the radio, ask about their listeners. Yes, even if it's a radio interview over the phone, dress appropriately for the audience. You've heard it said that a smile can be heard over the phone. Well, if you're dressed correctly, your voice will convey that as well.

Pride – Yes, you have every right in the world to be proud. You're an author. Use that pride to stand tall and take on the challenge of marketing yourself and your book and never, ever forget to pay it forward. Many helped you to get where you are. Many are still helping you reach your goals. Remember to take a look behind, reach out a hand and give another author a little help too. It's what makes Pride a virtue and not one of those ugly sins.

ASSIGNMENT

Is everything you need ready and polished? List your marketing tools and goals and decide what needs to be worked on.

Then take a serious look at your image. How's your appearance on Twitter and Facebook? How's your photo and bio? Have you updated your bio recently or perhaps forgotten to update it everywhere? Websites, Facebook, Twitter, LinkedIn … everywhere? How strong are your speaking skills and what can you improve upon?

This is an ongoing project and should be treated as such. Make a note on your calendar to check these things every few weeks or months, just to be sure your marketing tools are exactly as you want them to be. It's very easy to fall off track, but even easier to get back on if you're vigilant about your goals and how you plan to get there.

THE BEAUTY

The Beauty of Geisha Marketing

Do you hate Facebook? Despise Twitter? Do anything to avoid blogging or updating your author or book website? Worse yet, do you love these things so much you forget to actually write or prepare for your book's eventual release or ongoing, growing success?

There are things you must do in order to establish the groundwork for your marketing. The truth of the matter is that becoming a successful selling author is not for the weak or whiny.

Marketing is all about building an awareness of your product – your book. Creating a social network online and in the real world is the basis for the success you're seeking. There's something beautiful about bringing a dozen well developed marketing elements together and watching it bloom into something startlingly profitable. But, where do those elements come from? Where do they start and how do they get in place? The answer to those questions is simple. You.

Marketing Harmonies Outside of the Norm

Let's discuss the marketing harmonies outside of the norm. Most people think that social networking means sitting at a computer or cell phone screen and being clever in 140 character clips. Twitter is great, but it's not everything.

There's the great Twitter/Facebook face off. I've had authors tell me repeatedly that they get more results from one over the other, but here is the truth. You need to be present in both venues and more.

There's the complaint, "What do I say?" Seriously? You're writers! Are you trying to tell me you can't communicate with people? All right, that sounded a little harsh and I do understand that many authors are shy creatures. Without being even harsher, you do know what happens in nature, right? Survival of the fittest. How can a shy, quiet author become one of the survivors? There are several techniques.

Remember, in social networking, you can't just show up and pitch. You need to read other people's comments then respond. Interact. Once you get response you've begun a dialogue. Now you're making friends or fans or creating relationships with business associates you never met before. It's actually very easy. You can do it on Twitter and Facebook. You can even do it by responding to the blogs you read. You'll be amazed how quickly your follower or friend numbers grow, as well as how many new people begin to come and read your blogs.

Getting outside the norm means stepping away from the computer. Join groups. If your book is about birds or has a bird loving character in it, join bird watcher or bird discussion groups and meet-up gatherings. Create relationships with breathing human beings who may want to read your book, get to know the author, or just enjoy you for who you are.

Where does the harmony come in? If you can find six different venues for relating to prospective book buyers, venues filled with people who are interested in you and your genre or book subject, then you have created harmony. Develop a list of various networking resources you have. Dig deep into the book you've written to find your "hooks". Remember all the major elements of your book and focus on reaching readers interested in those elements. When you're working all six venues the music starts and it's beautiful as reflected in growing book sales.

And all this time you never once asked one person to buy your book!

Commitment

This one's big. You need to determine what you are willing to do for your success. You also need to understand that this isn't a winding road at all, it's a freeway as straight and clear as they come.

If you choose to use your Author Platform and/or Book Platform to mention that you're writing a second or third book in a series, you better follow through. If you mention at a writers or special interest (pertaining to your book) luncheon that you want to establish a 10K walk to help a related cause, get your calendar out and PEN it in. If you think you may want to begin a whole new book on a subject your readers stated they'd love to see from you, think hard before announcing it. Why?

Nothing is more counter-productive than leading a fan or reader down a wrong path. Only add or announce something in your platforms when you are positive. Don't over book yourself and never simply state that you "might" do anything. Your image is what you're holding like a picket sign when you market. If your image has several elements or events crossed off (even in the reader/fan's memory) you suddenly become one of those people. The kind no one believes because they never follow through. It may have happened just once and for a very good reason, but it is indelibly tattooed on the public's memory.

Commitment is something an author must take seriously. There are several things you are marketing here. Your book, your future books, you and your credibility. Make things easy and consider your commitments before stepping up to the plate.

Cultivating New Readers/Fans

Time to find and cultivate new lovers of your performance, because it's exactly what you need to be doing all the time.

The only way to do this is to clearly understand the market and specifically, your market. Take the field trip mentioned in the beginning of this book and get yourself to a major bookstore and just observe. If you write romance, root yourself in the romance section and watch buyers come and go. Watch how they react to certain book covers and subject matter. How many read the cover blurb before choosing a book? How many look at several books before choosing? How many go immediately to a specific author and tug the exact book they want then leave?

You want to create a desire among all of these kinds of buyers. They are the market and they are your market. That means that for the romance readers who have interest in flashy bright book covers, you need to reach them. For the readers who read a cover blurb first, you must be sure your blurb is spectacular. For the reader who comes looking for the author first and his/her newest book second, you'd better have a fantastic Author Platform.

You may already be successful with one or more of these particular buyers, but in order to grow your readership and fan base, you must seek out and market to the readers you don't have. If you do this, your back list will remain alive and hopping rather than a bunch of books no one ever buys anymore.

Another way to entice new fans is to find them where they are doing other things. If your book is a mystery, make sure you are connected with mystery reading groups, that you are reviewed by some of the larger mystery reviewers, and that you're visible at major mystery lovers groups or other highly visible mystery writer's events.

And finally, you need to market to prospective readers and fans where they least expect it. If your book's hero is a gardener, do a book event or book signing in a gardening store or at a beautiful city garden. If your book is a romance about a fireman, do your best to not only support firefighters, but perhaps do fundraisers through your book sales to help their efforts. If your book is about a particular part of a particular town or city, do a book event there. Market your books in places most people don't think about books. If your book is about a real estate executive, see if you can advertise in real estate companies' employee or (better yet) customer newsletter (online and hard).

The general rule of marketing is three exposures. THREE. If the same book buyer doesn't see you and your book in at least three different places, hear about it from three different sources, or get the scoop from three different friends or associates, you may not get the sale. You will have a much stronger chance at being successful if you are careful to market yourself and your book to the correct target – that is:

- Where they buy their books - in stores and online
- Where they think about books – in their reading clubs and peripheral book news
- And finally where they least expect to see a book – got tropical fish in your book? Get it visible in tropical fish stores.

Gaining new readers for your book(s) is a constant effort. Go on, stop for a few months and see what happens. Granted, after a while of being vigilant and active, you will have grown a massive following and you can leave the "gaining new readers" efforts to your huge reader base. But for now? You got it – it's your job.

ASSIGNMENT

Where will you find your "outside the norm" marketing harmonies? List SIX different and unique venues where you can reach prospective book buyers. Remember, this must be intimately based on your manuscript and a location or venue where you've never seen a book event held before. Is there a scene in your book that takes place in a laundromat? At a museum? Is there a critical plot twist that occurs at a riverbank? On a train or barge? Can you find prospective readers there or better yet, can you draw them there for an event? Perhaps you can post flyers or arrange for a speaking engagement someplace interesting and deeply influenced by your story.

Once you've listed your SIX different and unique marketing harmonies, begin to plan them and see how you can make them happen.

THE PERFORMANCE

The Performance of Geisha Marketing

The history of the Geisha starts somewhere around 1600 and still continues in some form today. This is one lengthy performance and teaches us all that the secret to survival is stability and durability backed with a whole lot of fortitude and endurance. How does this apply to an author? Take a look around.

In truth, you can count on your own fingers and toes the authors who have reached the pinnacle and remained there for over a decade. There are a thousand factors that contribute to this. The economy and current public attitude only plays a small part, believe it or not. Most of the authors on your top 20 list are probably still top 10 best sellers and still backed by their publishers all the way to the bank.

Now take a deep breath and step back. You are just beginning or only ankle deep in an industry that is quaking with massive changes. No one really knows how quickly e-publishing will take over. Now factor in the responsibilities authors must carry for their own success, and my fear is that in two decades, you might not be able to find as many successful long term authors at all – unless they all learn that the performance is a long, long one and they're playing many of the parts in this show.

Consistency, Continuity and Patience

Every author, no matter where they are in the process – just starting their first book, just getting their first agent or first book published, or moving on with further books – should have an effective Book Business Plan and a solid strategy for establishing goals and building success. A plan like that means taking some serious time to think long and hard about a whole career. If you thought that all an author had to do was write books, you're sorely mistaken. You can go ahead and do that, but without sales, why? The point of being an author and writing your book is to have people read it.

When an author tells me they're in this for the art, I can't tell you how hard it is to not simply cry for them. Granted, it hasn't completely ended yet and there are still some sterling six figure advances for extraordinary work by first-time authors. It's just a matter of the odds. We all want to believe we're going to be the one, but what does it hurt to be prepared? Have a plan? A strategy for success no matter what happens?

In fact, having that plan may look very good to a prospective literary agent or publisher. It just may tip the balance in your favor. Either way, being an author in control of your destiny and backed with a reality based plan can only make the entire experience that much better.

If you are consistent in your efforts to write the book, what happens? It gets completed, right? If you have a continuity of style and plot, your book not only gets done, it's pretty darn good. Now comes the hard part – patience. Few authors out there didn't wait and hope and pray on bended knee for a contract. These days there are more options, the big publishers, indie publishers, POD and e-publishers as well as self-publishing. No matter which way you go, you will need patience.

Now, let's apply those "virtues" to marketing.

- Consistency – Have a strong plan in place and never waver. If you're consistent, your reader base will grow and grow.
- Continuity – Never, ever drop off the face of the earth. You'd be amazed how many authors see the ball start rolling and take a few weeks away from Twitter, forget to blog for months, completely ignore their Facebook page and take a vacation rather than make appearances at writing groups or social gatherings. When the interest in their book falls off, they panic and there's no one to blame but themselves. Without practiced continuity, the reader won't be looking for your next book. They'll have simply forgotten about you.
- Patience – Along with patience, as you push your efforts ahead, you will need persistence with your marketing plan, a careful eye for alterations and adjustments and a great Book Business Plan to assure you're staying on course.

Now on to the actual marketing performances and how they work.

Short and Long Performances

As I said earlier, marketing is a powerful combination of promotion, publicity and networking, but it isn't any one of those things at all. To market, you and your book need to be branded, so doing your Author and Book Platforms well is vital. To market, you must already have a following. It's cool that you've done all your Twitter and Facebook friending. You've made yourself accessible and religiously blog something relevant every single week. Now is the time to start marketing.

Short Performances

Cross Marketing - How can you cross market? Will it work through blogging with another author or someone with a theme related to your book? Can you create an entire blog tour with all your fellow bloggers no matter what they blog about and write an entry that connects with your book?

Do you write zombies? Who else writes about zombies? Connect with them and create an entertaining cross marketing plan.

Is your book about downhill skiing? Connect with ski equipment stores to contribute to their online or hard newsletter for their customers. Good cross marketing is a two way road so always makes sure you've got some way to bring people's minds back to that store. For example, perhaps they can provide bookmarks that are also a 10% discount coupon for equipment purchase. You distribute the bookmarks, they display your book.

Is your book a non-fiction about obesity? Make the same cross marketing efforts with a health club or weight loss product.

No matter what your book is about, there is some complimentary industry to cross market with. Cross marketing is a great way to piggyback exposure and gain new contacts. Think hard, you can find and connect with the perfect cross marketing solution for your book. We'll be talking at greater length on Cross Marketing later in this book.

Real Life Marketing - How about in the real world? What can you do in the short term for your real life friends?

Never forget the "Home town kid does good" card. Using that can take you far. Get yourself booked in local libraries to do a reading or local indie book stores for events and signings.

Leave a small flyer or poster (with book cover picture and purchase information) everywhere that will post it: the local coffee shop, dentists offices, gyms and spas, grocery markets, clubs.

How about your local writers or authors organization? They love to post success stories in their news letters and are always thrilled to have a guest speaker. WARNING: many authors tend to connect heavily with other authors for all their marketing efforts. As supportive as the camaraderie is, this strategy for marketing is a little counterproductive. Look for marketing directions that are less competitive and directly connected with the book buyers you seek. The ratio is simple. For every author you're marketing with, you need to be marketing to 10 non-author, interest-related prospective buyer groups.

Be sure to tag all your emails with a line that tells your book title and a link for more information. Create email groups who are interested in your blog and keep them posted on your progress. You are an author, tell everyone!

Long Performances

Book Platform Strategies – Do you have a strategy? Or was your strategy simply to have a web presence? If so, you've fallen way short. Your Book Platform (whether a website or blog) must be a living, breathing thing. It must be updated regularly and I'm not talking once a quarter either. A weekly blog update does several things for you as an author. Google search engines will pick up on the fact that you, the author, have updated. It will also pick up your tags which should include your book title and genre. If you have a book website, don't forget about the poor thing. Update something there at least once every two weeks. There are hundreds of things you can do. You can post your "cutting room" scenes, those entire scenes that get chopped right out of your book. You can develop background on your characters. Post related real news stories. Create contests and more. All this can happen before you even have news to put into your Book Website Media Room. Having a book website is not simply a place to announce you have a book, it's the stage for performing to an audience. Besides, if you don't update regularly, what reason would there be for anyone to come to the website? We want them to return often, curious and excited to see what's new.

Author Platform Strategies – Everything mentioned above works here too, but the most effective and dynamic place to update your Author Platform (whether it's a website or blog) is in the Media Room. There you can announce new sales venues for the book, you can announce speaking engagements or interviews, you can talk about the fact that your book is raising money for a charity, or how you and your fellow authors are doing a 10K walk for cancer. You can always update your press photo or bio. No matter what you do, Google finds out, your ranking rises and again, readers visit often to see what's up.

The Long-term Overview – Nothing is temporary where marketing for yourself or your book(s) is concerned, except your career. To make it solid and keep it growing and alive, you must keep your long performances fresh and active!

Harmonious Presentation

Creating the harmonious presentation of yourself and your book(s) is all about taking your amazing, precise groundwork – all the exposure and awareness you created through marketing and publicity – and parlaying that into spectacular promotions. Unfortunately, it's a thousand times tougher to promote anything if no one knows it exists.

ASSIGNMENT

What are your short performances? What are your long performances?

Your short performances happen in bursts, just enough to get your message across then sit back and see how it works. Short Performances are something anyone can do and most authors do religiously.

What will make you stand apart is your Long Performances, so I strongly recommend you make your strategies an organized, religiously followed activity. Create a chart of your Long Performance elements and a check system, where you mark off each time you update these elements. For example:

Book Platform	*Wk 1*	*Wk 2*	*Wk 3*	*Wk 4*	*Wk 5*	*Wk 6*	*Wk 7*	*Wk 8*
Embedded blog	*yes*	*yes*	*yes*	*yes*	*yes*			
Character Studies	*yes*	*no*	*yes*	*no*	*yes*			
Media Room	*yes*	*yes*	*yes*	*yes*	*yes*			
Contest	*no*	*yes*	*no*	*yes*	*no*			
Letters	*yes*	*no*	*yes*	*no*	*yes*			

Under this Book Platform, the author will have a weekly embedded blog about her most recent book on that genre Book Platform website. She has character studies and updates every other week, just a sneak peek about each character's personality. She updates her media room every week with something, and makes sure every link is working perfectly. And finally, every other week she posts letters she receives from her fans along with answers.

Author Platform	Wk 1	Wk 2	Wk 3	Wk 4	Wk 5	Wk 6	Wk 7	Wk 8
Media Room	yes	yes	yes	yes	yes			
Charity update	yes	no	yes	no	yes			
Embedded Blog	yes	yes	yes	yes	yes			
Letters	no	yes	no	yes	no			

For the Author Platform, she takes care of her Media Room every single week, checking links and adding information. The author has a Charity Update, where she updates how much money she's raised for the charity connected to her book. She has an embedded weekly blog focused on making her the expert at the subject, craft or genre of her book. And finally, she posts letters regarding her charity, along with fundraising events taking place all over the country for that charity.

Keep a chart like this posted on the wall near your computer. Never miss a week and keep your Long Performances alive, exciting, informative and fun.

REPUTATION

The classic Japanese Tea Ceremony (The Way of the Tea) is all about preparation. It involves thoughtful action and special tools. It creates an environment where the participants are completely present in the moment.

The Marketer's "T" Ceremony has the same qualities. "T" stands for Testing. This is how it's done.

Tracking Success

Everything you do, from creating Book and Author Platforms to seeking out new and unusual venues for possible readers and book buyers is nothing more than a test. I've encouraged you to stretch the envelope, think outside of the box and fearlessly approach those new avenues. But how do you know if they're successful?

Of course, the bottom line tells all, but which marketing strategies worked better? Which are dogs? Which can be improved upon? Without some kind of testing plan, you'll never know if you're wasting your time on something weak and not taking advantage of something else that just may be working better. There are a few simple tools to help.

Coding – Coding your marketing approaches is easy. You can create codes with a special note or offer that can be easily traced. For example, doing your marketing to one specific group and having them comment on your blog in response to an upcoming event or specific question is good. This means that you've raised your awareness well and those readers are reacting exactly as you wish. You can also code by choosing a different group and offering them something different, a signed copy of the book or a free lesson with you on your area of expertise (i.e. your book is about a man out at sea, and ask the group to respond at your blog or on Twitter or Facebook about sailing. The winner gets a chance to discuss their adventures with you or you can answer their questions about sailing a particular part of the world. A contact who is a fan is a good person to know – the kind that gives you a ton of information about why people are buying your book that you never thought about.)

Contests – Again, in order to test the marketing strategy best, you'll need to choose a particular group. Say you write murder mysteries. You can create a "who done it" or "find the red herring" contest and reward the most creative answers with some prize. Perhaps you create a winners wall on your blog to acknowledge them. REMEMBER: this isn't promotion, this is all about testing your marketing. For example, if you've been exposing your book to a particular group and they don't respond, it's pretty clear that it's time to move on. Sometimes we want a particular collection of readers to like our book so much, we never test it, we simply hope that they are among the possible buyers or fans. The best "T" Ceremonies know to go where the power is. That's why we test, and test often.

Eliminate – Yes, simply eliminate a particular group from your general marketing strategy and see what happens. Was there a major drop in reaction? Or did everything stay the same?

The obvious key here is to seek out and heavily target the marketing strategies that are working best for you. Eliminate the ones that aren't. Time is valuable. Don't waste it if you don't have to. If you spend five hours every week writing guest blogs, and discover that these efforts are not getting you more awareness, take those five hours back! You can be writing other things – like your next book – with that time.

There's a poetry and timing to good testing. You should test your strategies every few months with something interesting and telling. Testing the market you are cultivating can only make it stronger. Don't be afraid, test away. You may learn some very interesting things about what you thought was working and what really works.

A simple example comes from my chef days. When analyzing a menu (which is a key restaurant marketing tool), everything is taken into consideration. Food cost, prep time and sales. It's uncanny how many times a chef discovers that his or her best selling item makes the least money. Of course, you don't always have to remove that item, you just need to restructure and re-engineer your physical menu. The items that take less time, labor and cost to produce (the most profitable) should be highlighted, and that costly, popular item should take a back seat.

Every industry tests their marketing strategy. So should authors. What you learn from your tests can be immensely valuable. How you tweak or change your approach is all up to you. Sometimes you just have to change the menu.

ASSIGNMENT

Tracking success and failure is far simpler than it sounds. It's done with three simple practices that should become second nature. Coding. Contests. And Elimination.

Create a stack of cards (maybe cut a few 3" X 5" index cards in half) and write as many ways as you can think of for coding your marketing efforts, one on each card. Do the same for contests, only in a different color ink. Put them in a "Coding" hat or "Contest" hat and when it's time to test a strategy, just pull a few out and rock your marketing. A few ideas for you to start

with can be:
CODING
- *Coding with a color (red alert, green meanie, blue zone)*
- *Coding with a number*
- *Coding with a password*
- *Coding by zip code or location*
- *Coding with a P.O. (Post Office) Box*
- *Coding by time or day, day of week, week of month*

CONTESTS

We all know how these work, just get creative and have a contest, rotate locations or times of day and test by code for best results. WARNING – be careful about giving away books. Yes you should give away a few, but don't be the one stop location for a free book every time you have a contest. Think of other swag or ideas for giveaway … perhaps an hour consulting to help another author with their plot, or maybe a box of cookies (just like the ones your main character loves) or even a Starbucks gift card.

ELIMINATION

Coding and testing your marketing only works if you analyze the results and determine if you received the response you wanted – more "Likes" on your Facebook FanPage, more sales, more visibility and/or demand for your next book.

Analyze deep. Yes, you got response, but did you get enough response? Are you happy with the results? Make notes on everything then eliminate all the strategies that didn't work.

Remember, just because a strategy did work, does not mean it will work forever, or that it will not get old and boring if the fans see it too many times. You need a variety of ideas and a variety of ways to target and code your strategies. You may discover that tweeting about a contest coded "red alert" on Thursday afternoons is better than Thursday mornings. There's no rhyme or reason to how a test will play out.

Elimination is the key to filling your bag with great ideas you know do work. Get rid of the duds no matter how much you like them or think they're cool. Only use the successful strategies and only test your marketing once every month or two. Too many contests get as boring as too few. Find the happy medium and note everything for future reference. Keep it all in a notebook beside your Coding and Contest idea hats.

A final note on marketing ideas and strategies – they will get stolen and used. Deal with it and by all means, be EVEN MORE creative and come up with the next great concept. Keep in mind that people remember the first time they saw or heard something, not the second or third.

MAKING YOUR MARKETING REALLY SING

"My biggest marketing effort to date is my character blog. "Too Picky ...? I Think Not!" is my character Molly Hacker's own blog. (www.mollyhacker.com) Every Monday, Molly blogs about everything and anything in her picky orbit. Every Wednesday, Molly, a reporter, also interviews a person of interest.

Not only do I spend a great deal of time on this effort, I have unique graphics created for each blog. As if putting all of this together was not enough, I then try to promote it as best I can, always looking for new and innovative ways to reach my audience. So far, it's showing real success in attracting fans for Molly Hacker."

~ Lisette Brodey, Author, "Molly Hacker is Too Picky!"

Part 5
ROMAN EMPIRE PROMOTION

"Any intelligent fool can make things bigger and more complex … it takes a touch of genius and a lot of courage to move in the opposite direction."

~ Albert Einstein, 1879 - 1955

BOOT CAMP

Publicity is using the media to create relevant exposure for your book. Marketing is building awareness that your book exists. So … what is Promotion? Promotion is the activity around which you sell your book! Note the word "activity". This is not something you can sit back and hope happens. Promotion is the action that makes the sales. Now, time for Boot Camp!

Understanding Goals

What are your goals? Yours, not another author's, or what you've heard an author's sales goals should be. What do you want from your book sales bottom line? Is it a number of books? A dollar figure? Prestige with a certain group of genre readers? Enough reader demand to have a reason to write the next book? What are your goals?

Identify them, define them and remember to give them growth opportunities as well as wiggle-room for shifting or changing. But before you set your goals, you'll need to understand the standard expectations. Those are slightly different for a variety of different kinds of books and readers as well as how the books are published.

I speak with dozens of authors over the course of a week. They are published across many genres and in all different formats. For the most part, an average ebook can expect to sell between 100 and 300 books on average over a 90 day period. If you want to surpass that, it can certainly be done, but you'll need to determine how far you want to surpass it before you can decide what strategies to use to attain your goal. Self published books have different standard average sales for fiction and for non-fiction. Small indie-published books with minimal distribution have yet another standard average sales number. Same for small publishers with fair distribution and the big publishing houses with large distribution.

Here's the kicker – they all seem to be close to the same. The difference between making big sales and falling into the average or low sales category is how, where, when and why you promote. Period. And remember, even if you are an author lucky enough to be published by one of the big publishers, if you don't show way above average sales, you might not get a chance to publish many more books with them.

It's all about the bottom line. Sales. Yes all writers are artists, but without sales, we're artists without a place to show our work.

Setting goals is a challenge to yourself, and I'm going to say something you may not have heard before, but I strongly suggest that you set those goals through the roof. Caution is not prudent in this situation because it costs nothing to aim high. And besides – since most authors are still slugging around in the dark ages, wearing blinders and thinking someone else (their agent or publisher) will manage to get their book sold – this battlefield is big and lush and ripe for the picking! An author who understands how to set goals, strategize and promote to gain sales is way ahead of the game. If they also understand how publicity and marketing work, they've got all the tools for success.

All an author needs beyond that is a little excitement and a lot of courage. Gird your loins, it's time for battle!

Getting Your Product Battle Ready

Your book is your product. If you owned a candle store and your product was candles, how would your candles look? Would you leave them all hidden in boxes, stacked along the aisles and unopened? Would you paint your little shop for ambiance and display the candles? Would you go as far as to burn a few candles, showing off the wonderful scents and inviting customers in by the nose? All three tactics work, but it's not hard to guess which candle shop owner will do better business.

Getting your product in shape for battle is about more than having a great cover and wonderful blurb. It's about more than great editing and genre marketability. Getting your product in shape for battle is about more than just getting a few books in your hands or facing your keyboard armed with a buy link at Amazon. Amazon and wherever you may be selling/signing your hard book is not promotion. It's not even battle. It's simply making your product available.

Battle is about being more than available. It's about being desirable. Did you all get a flashback to the senior prom? Yeah, it's like that, only we're far more ready to win this time. It's not the football quarterback or homecoming queen we're trying to gain, it's readers by the hundreds … thousands … dare we say … millions.

Battle Ready Check List

- Is your Book Platform active, alive and rocking?
- How is your Author Platform? Is it up to date and reaching out?
- Have you used publicity and marketing to create exposure for and awareness of your book?

- Have you created lists, groups and contact venues (live and online) to make announcements and request events for your book?
- Have you made your Twitter and Facebook friends aware of your book launch? Have you made your live, offline friends aware too?
- Are you constantly seeking new ideas, twists on ideas and promotional strategies for your book? Are you observing and improving on other promos you've seen? Are you using your "hooks" for deeper success?
- Have you built a loyal fan base? It can be small but it must be loyal and aching to grow.

Okay, don't panic. We'll be discussing and developing all these concepts in this section and before we're done here, you will have a nice, big red checkmark beside every item on this list.

Reviewing the Troops and Tightening the Machine

Who are your troops? The troops could be you and only you, or you and your fictitious characters. It could be you and your best friend who builds and maintains your websites. It could be you and your mom, family and close buddies who want to see you succeed. Your troops are those you know will stand by you and trust with your life. Your network. Troops include:

Personal assistant or someone who always steps up and says, "Oh hey, I can do that for you." Never refuse genuine help. You can't do it all and as you move closer to the promotional phase of your author journey, you need all the help you can get.

Techies, Twitter followers and Facebook friends. Believe it or not, if you're not always asking for help, when you do, these amazing people always step forward with suggestions, ideas and even contacts. Sometimes you get nothing, but you're not being ignored, you may have simply chosen the wrong time or the wrong day of the week to ask. For example, on Twitter, watch the stream for a while before hopping in. Who's there? Are they your regular friends? Is it later or earlier than you usually tweet? Is it the week of a holiday, day before a holiday or week after a holiday? Is it summer vacation time? Your most active interactors on Twitter and Facebook live real lives just like we do and are probably acting or reacting in line with whatever time of the day or season it is. Strategically use Twitter and Facebook for best response when requesting information or recruiting help.

Your network of authors. They too are facing the daunting task of promotions, or perhaps they've successfully won that battle. Either way, keep your network close. If only for advice or to help you keep your sanity over a cup of coffee, your support network is important.

Your troops also include (are you ready?) YOUR STORY, CHARACTERS AND BOOK SUBJECT. If you don't already know this, you may be behind the eight ball. Come on out, it's not too late. As we've discussed throughout this book, the success to your career as an author lies not only in you - but in your book. The one you've already written (or almost finished). Your book genre, subject and characters are your biggest warriors because, as with real troops, your entire battle is based on them. The promotional strategies are created around them, your audience is drawn from them and your creative plan is derived from them. If your book is about an erotic romance that happens in an abandoned West Virginia coal mine, it's not likely your promotions will revolve around children making glitter pictures about rainbows and puppies. It's a drastic comparison but you would be surprised how many authors create promotions that have little to do with their story. Your story is the fertile ground for all your promotional ideas. Stray far from there and you will be lost and bloodied.

What is the machine? The machine is the timing, strategy and stamina of your promotional plan. If the machine is rusty, manned badly or without fuel, we've got a problem. An author who wants to write a book and loses steam halfway through usually doesn't finish that book, right? They've lost interest in the subject or characters or plot or even genre. It's dead. The same thing can happen to a promotional plan.

This is the reason all elements of Publicity, Marketing and Promotion must be generated by the author through the story that author has written. You know what's in your story. You know how it can be made relatable to a reader, a promotion, an event, a sales goal. YOU, and no one else.

I have no issues with authors wealthy enough to hire marketing professionals, promotional experts and publicists. I just worry that they may not be getting the best marketing, promotions or publicity they can. Once an author has made the grade, risen to be the General of their army and becomes a terrific promotional strategist, yes, I can see passing the work on to the professionals. The land has been laid and it's clear what that author writes and who they reach.

But in the beginning it's actually a blessing to have control over such things. You are a creative individual. You've written a book with a unique story, amazing characters and plot. Now all you have to do is get a little more creative and promote with the same gusto! When your machine is fueled with strong, connected ideas, workable promotional plans and based on established marketing and publicity, you will win.

CAESAR STRATEGY VS. WAR OF THE WORLDS

Caesar Strategy vs. War of the Worlds. I can hear you now. "Huh? What is she talking about?" But trust me, this makes a lot of sense.

All battles, large and small, play themselves out on the same criteria and they all get critiqued after the fact. The enemy wants something, the defender wants something else. Clash! George Washington? Great strategist? The experts say no. Julius Caesar? The experts say, hell yes!

H.G. Wells created something elegantly fictitious back in 1897 when he wrote War of the Worlds. On October 31, 1938, Orson Welles headed a live radio broadcast production of the same story that intensely scared listeners everywhere.

The strategies are the same. Success is about making an impact and gaining control. Julius Caesar did it, and so did Orson Welles. They did it differently but do you know what their biggest, most powerful strategy for attaining their goal was?

Promotion. Julius Caesar's greatest skill wasn't how quickly or efficiently he could take territory for Rome, it was in how boldly he showed the terrified enemy that he could take them. He had savvy and bravado and used it to simply scare the crap out of the Germainians and Gauls. Then, of course, he went in and captured it all, but his power was in making it clear that he could, whenever he wanted.

Orson Welles' promotional conquest was quite different. There's an entire promotional practice called 'teasers'. Teasers are sort of like whispered bits of information, or whispered bits of strategic mis-information. The tactic is geared toward perking the ears of a possible buyer and sucking them in with intrigue. In 1980, the book Shogun by James Clavell was made into a television miniseries here in the States. I'd already read the book nearly a year earlier but when the teaser promos began on television, I was hooked without even realizing what I was hooked onto. There was no title, no list of actors, no clear statement that it was a television mini-series or a film. Just the 10 second black background, the sound of metal against metal, and the shimmering Samurai blade. I, along with many viewers, was enthralled.

The teaser works its magic by tantalizing and playing with the prospect. It's not bait and switch, it's the sharp hook without the whole bait.

Welles did this with his Broadcast of War of the Worlds not only as a mis-information teaser to get people to tune in, but also as an overall layer of presentation. That's why so many believed that the world was actually being taken over by alien spacemen.

Where Caesar stood tall and looked down his nose at his next conquest from high places, Welles simply snuck in under cover of darkness. These are only two of many strategies for promotional success.

Reviewing the Battlefield

Which way do you go? Teaser? Blatant threat? Or any of a hundred other effective strategies? There's only one way to make an educated strategic decision. Know the battlefield.

Four Elements to the Solution

<u>**Your Genre.**</u> Let's imagine you've written a Romance. Is it a genre romance? Paranormal romance? Erotic romance? Historical romance? Maybe you've written a mystery? Does it play out in a humorous landscape? A historical, military, period or fantasy landscape? All these things are important because your first line of attack is always one of reconnaissance.

How many other books out there fall directly into your genre category? How many authors are extremely successful in sales within that specific genre category and how many mid-list or minor authors manages to appear under that category? Understanding all this is vital because if you don't know the battlefield, you can't fight efficiently.

It's not terrible to imitate a successful strategy, but it is counter-productive and foolish to recreate someone else's successful promotional campaign. Trust me, you'll look like a hack and after all, who really remembers the second person to do anything? Name the second person to fly around the world, the second man to go into space, the second brand of sports drink to hit the market. You can't. Why? You don't remember because it wasn't important. The mark was already made.

If you discover or witness an amazing promotion, digest it, dissect it and then rebuild it completely as your own. One way to find wonderful, successful promotions to help you create your own, is to look outside of the publishing world. Was there a city event promotion with a twisted theme that caught your attention? How can you use the bones of that promotion to promote your book? Do you recall a fantastic commercial that never left your mind? Can you use the concept for your book?

The bottom line is that how you create your own signature promotional strategy must begin within your genre. If the promotional idea has never been done in your genre, you may have a winner. If it has, you will have a lot of work to do to make it your own. If you find something in another promotional arena that you simply can't fit into your genre audience appeal, walk away. Reconnaissance is about seeing what everyone else (and I mean everyone else, even non authors) is doing so you can do it better, different and more effectively for your own advantage.

Your Goals. You've set your goals, now it's time to use your amazing imagination. Take a full day and sit quietly to think. Based on the battlefield and what other successful authors are doing, begin your examination. If you implement one particular promotional direction, take it to the limits inside your head. Take it right, left, up and down. Look at it from every angle. Think about how it can work, and what the consequences might be if it doesn't. Does it offer all the solutions or present a few problems? Are the problems manageable? Jot everything down and move on to the next promotional idea, then the next and the next. When you've finished, your notes should clearly tell you which idea you feel most confident with. It will reach your goals, win the war and put you on the map. You have become Julius Caesar because you thought and planned before you struck.

Your Story/Plot. Yes. Everything you need to be a successful selling author is right there in your manuscript. Let me repeat that because so many authors simply don't get this. Everything you need to be a successful selling author is right there in your manuscript.

If your book takes place in a futuristic post-apocalyptic world and you decide to do a promotion that focuses on inner city gardens, you may have missed the mark, unless the theme of your plot is the desperation of the characters to grow food. If your book is about werewolves trying to protect their young from being taken into animal shelters and you build your promotions around supporting animal shelters, you just may have something. Your story and plot are vital to creating the bond between your promotions, your book and the prospective buyer. It would be a terrible shame if your book is about antique bicycles but your promotion is built around the space program. No connection means no sales. Seriously. Incorporate your story elements powerfully into your promotions. This is how you take the standard battlefield and make it your own.

Your Courage. Be brave, you can do this. A coward never wins. Okay. Enough with the clichés, simply know the battlefield and build your book elements as a viable warrior. You will be fine. I promise.

Strategies Planned Around, Through and by Taking Advantage of the Enemy

Having taken your genre, goals and story/plot in hand, sharpened and polished them to use as tools to build your own promotional strategy on a battlefield you now understand, it's time to think about the enemy.

Okay, they're actually not the enemy but they are your competition. Who is the best, biggest selling and most highly visible author in your genre? How long have they been writing? On the Best Sellers List? Do you admire this author? Is your book jumping off from theirs or in direct response to their work? A contradiction? A bold variation?

Identify your direct one-on-one enemy and do a serious comparison. Of course, none of us are Barbara Kingsolver or Neal Gaiman, yet. But if you can see them as your direct competition in the genre, you can get there. This is the place where I tell you to take all your writer insecurities and toss them out the window. They don't serve you. It's time to be the master and plot your success.

Doing a serious comparison requires a bit of research. Where did your favorite author start their career? How did their first book get published? How did their second book play off the first? How were they marketed?

Now, don't do the standard author whine here! Don't sit back and toss up your hands before you even start. Don't sob and cover yourself with ashes because your favorite author is published by a huge publishing house and you can hardly get favorable responses from literary agent queries. We're not exploring your target's luck vs. your luck, or building a failure case based on what they have vs. what you don't have. We're taking a serious look at where they are so that we can study the steps they took to get there.

This information isn't so hard to find. Author Barbara Kingsolver wrote a collection of essays entitled High Tide in Tucson some years ago, and in it she has a few essays covering her journey as an author; what she did, how she did it and why she did it. She even explored whether she liked the process or not. Kingsolver is on the best selling list every time she releases another book. She also spreads herself around as an author. She writes everything from literary to exploratory to historical fiction. Where did she start? With a sweet series of novels about a woman's journey. That is the story of success. She didn't start with an attitude. She didn't play with ridiculous expectations. She wrote strategically and followed the guidance given to her by her publishers.

NOTE: Here's where I warn you all to remember that the times, they are a changin'. The publishing world is altering and the industry landscape is shifting constantly these days. What Kingsolver (or Dan Brown or Neal Gaiman) did was under another regime, a different Caesar with different weapons. Authors like John Locke and Amanda Hocking found their success in a completely different way than Gaiman or Brown, so it's wise to examine many different author's paths. Ebooks are the future and it's coming fast! So fast, that the future is almost yesterday. *The New York Times* has created a best seller list for ebooks. That says a lot. If you're traditionally published, you're probably also e-published. If you're seeking publication or just starting with your career, e-publishing may very soon become the only way to be published. Amazon announced recently that the digital book has taken over paper book sales on amazon. com. That's a big deal. How we promote on this new battlefield is going to be critical to our success. But don't ever forget that good promotion is good promotion. How you manage your promotions is what will put you on top.

Giving Orders

When you've done all your homework, understand the battlefield as it stands today, who your competition is and how they gained their status, you're ready to develop your own strategies for success. You can take great ideas and build them into great promotions. It will then be time to shout "At my signal, unleash hell!"

THE GENERAL SAYS ...

Who is the General? You are the General. Seriously.

As authors, facing rejection daily or struggling to find footing in this vacillating market, it's so easy to forget that we control our own destiny. We've all heard the lectures – plan your work and work your plan, dress for the job you want, constantly educate yourself for success.

They all apply here just as they do for an office job. Granted, personality comes into play. So many authors are withdrawn, preferring to sit alone at their computers, but I'm going to say something that may seem cruel here so please take it as tough love.

If you don't do these things to promote your book, you don't want success bad enough. As an Author Success Coach, I work constantly with authors who want to argue with me that they simply can't overcome shyness or their preferred image of the classic reclusive author and step outside their comfort zone to promote. Guess what? They will fail. It's that simple. There are many thousands of authors out there and literally many more thousands of books, good, bad and mediocre, coming out every single year. If you don't do what you have to do to stand apart and above, if you don't gird your loins and push the envelope, you may as well hang it up right now.

What? You're still here? Good. So now, let's get down to brass tacks. You are the General, you plan the battle strategy. Be a Patten, not a Custer. Know what you're up against and know how to win. This isn't about ego, it's about knowledge and strategy. If you're doing this right, your publicity is in play and your image is sharp. Your market awareness has laid the groundwork. Now your promotions will help you gain ground for success.

How Big is Your Staff?

No one does it alone. Whether you read books on how to write a great novel, how to create a wonderful non-fiction proposal or how to make friends and influence people, you've already begun to amass your staff. You are active on Facebook and Twitter so you have access to amazing professionals who are actively giving away free golden nuggets of information every single day. They're part of your staff. You have writer friends at various levels who have seen successes and failures and are always ready to pass on good information. They're on your staff. The television, radio, internet, newspapers and magazines are your staff of informants. Billboard promotional ideas are on your staff. All these virtually free staff members constantly offer valuable information to help you build your strategy.

There are the few authors who can afford to hire professionals. Be careful, read every word of an agreement before signing the bottom line with a publicist, marketing specialist or promotions manager. Make sure you are in control of your image at all times.

If you have a literary agent or promotionally savvy publisher, put them on your executive staff. They're in the trenches, they read the trades we aren't privy to and they can and will pass great tips and information on to you. They want to do this, after all, if you are successful, so are they.

Friends who have nothing to do with writing or your book are also resources. Next time you're at Starbucks or having lunch with a friend or business associate, listen when they talk about the things that influence them. This is a hidden gold mine of tips for effective promo planning.

Now, take inventory of your staff. There are tons of informed ideas floating under the surface of all that chatter. Learn how to manage the info and apply it to your promotional strategy.

Perfecting Strategies on Singular and Multiple Levels

There's the by-the-book way to promote anything from popcorn to the whole circus. There are standard procedures for promoting everything from movies to local theatre in the park. You need to understand those procedures. You need to watch everything going on around you and figure out what may or may not work for your book.

I'm sure you've heard the saying – There's more than one way to skin a chicken. Being a retired chef, I can attest to that in the culinary world, and being an author, I can attest to that in the promotional world.

There are literally hundreds of ways to approach the market on multiple levels but for now, good book promoters approach this challenge from three distinct directions.

- Play the "Genre Game"
- Approach a secondary audience
- Utilize public relations as a tool to help promotions

The "Genre Game"

We touched on this earlier but it's worth another brief run. No matter how you are published, who publishes you or what agent represents you, they will require a pigeonhole for your book. This isn't meant to be limiting, it's simply practical. If you go to a big book store and you want to buy a romance, you go to the Romance Section. If you are looking around an online store or Amazon for a paranormal book with some handsome vampires, you look under Paranormal. If you are interested in a story about a woman's journey, you check out the Women's Fiction category. Genres are designed to help book sellers lead readers to your book.

Now, to play the genre game. Let's say you wrote a paranormal book about a reluctant female werewolf who finds love with a handsome veterinarian. Understanding that the merchandising world must put your book into a category, probably the Paranormal category, doesn't mean that you can't reach out and promote to readers and audiences who may like your book even if they don't always frequent the Paranormal department. Now, how many categories can we say the book can be promoted within? 1) Paranormal. 2) Paranormal Romance. 3) Urban Fantasy. And 4) Women's Fiction.

What we're looking at now is the opening up of additional targets to promote to. Granted, the subgenre of Paranormal Romance may still be a tight readership, but adding romance to your promotional goals is a good strategy.

NOTE: When pitching literary agents or publishers, you NEVER want to play the "Genre Game". Stick to the standards and pitch your book genre as the query recipient wishes to see it. The "Genre Game" is in your hands for marketing and promotional strategies after the book is published.

Tapping into a Secondary Audience

This is where you look inside your manuscript where all your solutions are waiting. Is your main character a cop? A hair dresser? A soldier? See, no matter what your main character is, you should approach readers interested in that character's lifestyle. For example, if your main character is a serious coffee lover or owns a coffee shop, is there a way to contact coffee shop websites and ask to promote your book on the site with a buy link? If your character loves to cook meals at home and entertain, why not join a few online cooking and entertaining groups?

Join, make friends, and casually in discussion, you can mention that your main character in your novel had a great recipe for pound cake.

I'm sure that if you take a good look at your manuscript, you will find several viable secondary audiences and a mess of ways to reach them. Sometimes promotion isn't about making a big bang, sometimes it's about making the right connections with the right prospective book buyers. It's sort of like clustered firecrackers. Bam, bam, bam!

Public Relations as a Tool

Now publicity and public relations is a completely different approach to exposure than promotions, and you certainly can use a good publicity approach to help you gain visibility. Is there a charity that relates to your story/manuscript or non-fiction subject?

The paranormal novel about the werewolf and the veterinarian has a built in charity, animal rescue organizations. Some novels and non-fiction books take a little more digging, but trust me, it's all right inside your manuscript. It's part of the story you wrote. What charity connects best with your book? Did someone struggle with cancer in your book or receive a kidney transplant? Will the American Heart Association or the National Literary Council seriously connect with your book? If so, (and here's the easy part) you simply make sure that you tell the world that a percentage of all your book sales goes to that charity. Notify the charity that you're doing this. Make contact with the local chapters of the charity and ask them to post your support in their website or newsletters. Put the charity's logo on your website, your blog, in your email signature and on the back cover of your book. Many people are so emotionally connected with a particular charity they'll happily purchase your book to be a support. That new, originally unthought-of fan now opens a whole new universe of fans to your books. Besides, doing something good is good karma. And good karma always pays.

Visualizing Success

Do some serious visualization, but be creative with it. For example, don't visualize that your first book will be picked up by a huge publishing house and immediately land on the top ten best seller lists all over the world. That's a bit of leap-frogging and isn't productive. Do some practical visualization.

In your visualization, apply everything you want to do to make yourself successful. See yourself implementing promotional strategies. Go to your favorite online or real book store and look right at the very spot where your book will be. Feel the checks in your hand as sales grow. See yourself plotting your next book along with your next promotional efforts and imagine building them on the successes from your last book. Visualize success the way it really happens a step at a time.

And do these visualizations every single day.

"Strategy for success: rise early, work hard, strike oil."
~ J. Paul Getty, 1892 - 1976

THE SYSTEM OF BATTLE

Let's get right down to the nitty gritty. There's a system to everything and being unprepared or half-prepared is not in that system. Step back and take a serious look at all your efforts so far.

- Your Book Website is up-to-date and alive.
- Your Author Website updated is active and creating constantly growing membership. It has a Media Room. That Media Room is focused on the appropriate author information and the elements are easily downloadable.
- You understand your Platforms targets clearly – those targets are a collection of admiring friends, family and authors, but far more heavily represented by readers of your genre.
- You have a plan for managing your platforms as you get busier. You control your Twitter and Facebook time, blog appropriately – not too little or too much. There are strategies in play to assure you have time to do other things like do live events and/or write.
- You regularly explore your competition's active approaches to the market, their interviews, their platforms, their publicity and marketing exposure.
- You're always paying attention to the market and activities in your genre.
- You're watching the industry as it shifts and changes.
- You're always planning your future strategies.
- You're testing all your current strategies for effectiveness.
- You watch your sales numbers and compare them to the previous quarter, making sure that you can identify which activity has created more sales and which activity has fallen flat.

Without knowing and managing all of the above active and passive activities, you are at a great disadvantage when you actually plan or try to implement your promotional strategy. Don't forget, a promotional strategy isn't a promotion or two. It's not a collection of random approaches to the market. A promotional strategy is a major plan with interlocking and ongoing promotions. It is wave after wave of attacks, all carefully scheduled and interlaced.

Creating an effective strategy means that everything you need to make the best mark on the battlefield is in place. Take some time to check and double check your active and passive activities. Be sure that whatever promotional strategy you devise can be supported and carried through those activities.

Careful Timing

Some common sense applies here. If your book is a Christmas Holiday collection of short stories or a novel related to Valentine's Day, timing means everything. But there's more to timing than the obvious.

Keep your eyes on the competition. Watch the publishers' websites and online catalogues. Is a competitive publisher releasing a book similar to yours in March? Should you try to push for a February release, or sit tight until May?

It's so vital to keep your eyes peeled and ears perked. There's a whole world living and breathing and going on beyond an author's computer screen. Most authors are in tune with the current affairs, but watch out for major events that could make or break your book. For example, if your novel is about a major earthquake and weeks before its scheduled release, there actually is a disastrous earthquake, you may want to reconsider your release date. On the other hand, if your book is about 2012 and the end of the world, hurry and get that thing finished and published, because there are only 12 months in 2012 that will be a boon for your novel.

On the same train of thought, keeping an eye on what's going on around us can also help from the other end of an author's spectrum. Has something occurred that could be a remarkable concept for a new novel? Taking this route can be very interesting because not only can you get the charge of writing a new novel that you are sure will sell, but you can blog, write articles, short stories and interact on various online and live groups on the up-front and current subject, thus become the expert as the aftermath of the event evolves. Voila, an instant platform.

Just like comedy, promotional timing is everything, regardless from which angle you look at it.

THE CONQUEROR'S RESPONSIBILITY

Determining Success or Failure

No one but you can determine what a success or failure actually is. It's based on your personal goals and desires, and built on your personal efforts. If one author feels extremely successful meeting modest goals and inspired by the interest shown in their book, that's success. If another author wants 100,000 of their books sold in a short period and reaching 99,000 feels like a failure, then they have failed. One thing is a constant no matter what your goals and aspirations are as an author.

Desire + Effort + Knowledge = Results

There's simply no other way to say it. We could be talking about baking 20 dozen cookies or raising kids or being a successful author. It's all the same.

Watch your progress carefully. Remember that your strategies must be fluid and shift when necessary. A soldier in hand-to-hand combat isn't thinking about just their own next move, they're anticipating their enemy's next move. Watch the market shifts and remember it's an industry in flux. Change your tactic when it's called for and always remember that you are the Commander. You run the show.

Planning for the Future Empire

One of the most important things for you to do in this entire process is to document everything. When a promotional campaign is over, analyze, discover which elements worked or didn't work – how effective they were or could have been, and how necessary they were in the first place. Take inventory of what you did and what you received for those efforts. Look at the bottom line. Did you reach your goals? Are you happy with what you accomplished, how you did it and more importantly, would you do it again?

Everything you did is now a strategy to be studied and analyzed. Now you're a real General and you can see what you need to do to make the next campaign better.

Planning for your next book promotion is a matter of building on the success of your last book promotion and constantly watching the battlefield. Sometimes the answer to bigger success is as simple as changing the route you take to the battlefield – more push for your ebooks or new directions to promote your series or a different audience altogether. Sometimes the answer is to stick with the plan and just push a little more. Sometimes you just need to keep on going.

Always remember one thing, it's far easier to build one success on another than to try to build a success on a failure. Planning for your future books means knowing what is working and not working for you.

"Sometimes by losing a battle you find a new way to win the war."

~ Donald Trump

ASSIGNMENT

Review the battlefield. Do your reconnaissance and make your report. This way you'll have a clear idea of what you're are up against and how you plan to go to battle. Keep a running notebook loaded with information like this:

- *Competitor #1's Book: Top Seller, major publisher (Penguin), beautiful cover, distribution in bookstores and ebook, same genre but 12th book in the genre, well established. Fantastic platforms, expensive. No book video. Twitter active but no Facebook.*
- *Competitor #2's Book: Midlist, fourth book, Published by mid-sized publisher, dull cover, same genre but first time for author in this genre, promoted through publisher, nothing extra in her platforms. Book video is well known. Facebook active.*
- *Competitor #3's Book: New, first time author, indie-published, great cover, same genre, has no media room but great book website. Nice but not so popular book video. Twitter, Facebook active.*
- *Genre: All competitors considered Romance with Paranormal subgenre but none have character and plot twist similar to mine. None can cross market into additional subgenres that I can, (Time Travel, Steampunk, and Military)*
- *Goals: To approach on level field with competitors then break away with major promotions featuring my additional subgenres. To watch competitor's activity and slip in when they're quiet until my promotions are strong enough to directly compete. To reach promo sales levels and match the best seller competitor.*

Part 6

CROSS MARKETING MAGIC

WHAT IS CROSS MARKETING?

I've touched on this subject in several of my workshops and speaking engagements – and mentioned Cross Marketing in both the Book Business Plan and the Platforms Building sections of this book. Now it's time to dedicate some exclusive focus on Cross Marketing for authors.

Cross Marketing is magic, but it's no mystery. It isn't some surreptitious passworded process where you need to know the secret handshake or swallow live gold fish to learn the tricks. It isn't something only highly educated and experienced professionals use when you pay them boatloads of money to make you famous. Cross Marketing is simple and you can do it all by yourself. It's a way of finding multiple markets for your book, no matter the genre or basic target reader. It's a way of diving into your manuscript to mine new readers you never thought about. It's a way to develop an instinct about writing your next book that allows you to build in a few viable markets other authors may not have thought about. After all, isn't that the ultimate goal? To gain more readers, more followers, more fans?

Your book is your product and as grand as it is to reach the standard reader – mystery lovers for your mystery, or paranormal lovers for your werewolf adventure – it's even more exciting to see your readership expand and grow into areas you (and other authors) hadn't originally imagined.

We're talking creative, financial and emotional gratification here and all you need to do to expand your fan base is follow a few strategies.

THE CROSS MARKETING STRATEGIES

Mastering the simple strategies for cross marketing isn't difficult. Every industry in the world, no matter what they produce, does the same thing. There's no reason why authors shouldn't take advantage of these simple processes. In this section we'll be covering:

- Cross Marketing, from the obvious to the sublime
- Crossing the line into TURBO creative thinking
- Taking your platforms to even more effective places
- Locating your alternative markets
- How to approach cross markets
- How to maintain new markets
- A cross marketing worksheet

Nothing here is scary or too difficult for an author, after all, you developed a fantastic idea, wrote a whole book and managed to find publication. You can do anything! You're already a successful writer, now it's time to become a wealthy one. It is possible!

FROM THE OBVIOUS TO THE SUBLIME

I call Cross Marketing the Author's Magic because it's so simple and easy. Cross Marketing has been used by just about every other industry in the world since the beginning of marketing. P.T. Barnum used it to get as many different kinds of people as possible into the big top to see his shows, and you can use it to get as many different readers into your book too.

Let's start with a simple, non-book subject.

Imagine you've just inherited a pizza oven and rented the perfect little location on a high foot-traffic neighborhood street. You're going to make pizzas. Woo hoo! You're going to be rich! Everyone loves pizza, right? Nope. Believe it or not, not everyone out there loves red sauce, pepperoni and melted mozzarella cheese. You're barely making ends meet and need to gain more customers or you'll be out of business. You have a competitor a few blocks down the street so you go take a look at what they're doing. They're serving the same kind of pizza and they're hopping everyday. So what's the problem?

The problem is that your competition has been established and has loyal followers. What's a pizza marketer to do? Cross Market.

The first thing you do is take a look at who loves pizza:

- Young adults
- Young working parents who love it for the convenience
- Pizza aficionados who scour the city for the best pizza
- Foodies who seek the unusual
- Health buffs and vegetarians
- Kids

Now you look at why they go to a specific pizza shop:

- Is it for the price point?
- Is it for the quality?
- Is it for the uniqueness of the service or atmosphere?

It's time to look for ways to bring in more than the few customers you have while making sure to return the loyalty to those who have started to come to your shop regularly.

Let's take this one target at a time:

- Young adults - Protect the price points and look for things those young adults love in other parts of their life. Perhaps you can have a Teen Hour where the music is loud and fun and there are contests for those young people to enter to win a free pizza party or tickets to rock concerts.
- Young working parents - Maybe it's a good idea to have a special line for taking phone, text or fax orders so that the pizzas are ready for pick up or delivered at the perfect time.
- Pizza aficionados - Perhaps you can create a competition between all the local pizza places to raise money for a charity, kind of like American Idol only with pizza. That will get the aficionados' attention.
- Foodies - If you've decided this is a lucrative customer, you'll need to add special foodie items to your menu. Toss some fresh basil or rosemary into your pizza dough, top the pizza with unique sauces and ingredients. Maybe add a dessert pizza, something with a whipped cream cheese sauce topped with fresh seasonal fruits and sprinkled with chunky crystallized sugar.
- Health Buffs and Vegetarians - This requires healthy menu choices that cater to those customers. Take an online course on nutrition to help you plan the perfect menu items.
- Kids - Like McDonalds, you can do a few kid-friendly things. Offer catered kid parties, have kid-sized personal pizzas on the menu, design the little pizzas with a pepperoni smiling face.

Next you must make sure all those new targets know about your activities to serve them:

- Walk around and give away discount coupons targeted to each of your new menu features.
- Give away free sample bites to everyone who walks in.
- Take kiddie pizzas to one of the local little league games for the players to enjoy.
- Place an add in the local foodie, health buff and vegetarian publications.
- Make sure your signage lists your weekly events and who those events are targeted for so that passers-by can see it and make note.

You've taken your pizza shop and reached six new highly targeted customers than you originally had.

As you know, anyone can make a pizza, good, bad or boring – and in this day and age, anyone can write and publish a book, good, bad or boring. The competition for the book buyer's dollar is big so making sure you reach as many audiences as possible is one of the great keys to success. You have strong, long-established competition right in your genre. You have difficulties with reaching new book buyers and you have the same challenges the pizza shop has. But, as you can see, it's all about what's on the pizza – or in the book – that makes the difference.

Genre Games (The Obvious)

Let's say you've written a romance. Everyone loves romance, right? Maybe. But just setting up shop, just announcing that your romance is being released won't be enough. Of course you will reach the avid romance readers digging around for new authors but will that be enough?

Start with your subgenre. Is it paranormal romance? Is it YA romance? Is it erotic romance? Does it have a mystery in it making it a cozy or hot mystery romance of sorts? Playing the genre game is very important when planning your cross marketing strategies.

For example, there are ways to stretch the limits of a genre. Granted, for sales purposes on websites and in book stores as well as seeking an agent, you better be very clear on the genre, but think about what happens beyond that and who out there might love your book.

If your book is an urban fantasy with romance in it, why can't you market to romance readers? If your book is about romance with a werewolf, there's no reason you can't cross market that paranormal romance with general romance. We're talking about subtle approaches here, not slam-bam crashing into the door of a traditional romance reader's book club and insisting they'll love your book. There's a careful strategy to approaching cross market targets and that's not it. Research carefully. If a book club or reading group or even a book reviewer specifically says they want romance, dig deeper. You'll discover that romance is romance and falls under several genres. The key here is to reach readers your primary genre isn't reaching.

The Meat (The Sublime)

For this strategy, it really doesn't matter what your genre or subgenre is. This strategy is completely determined by WHAT'S INSIDE YOUR BOOK. You wrote this book and even though you may not have known it at the time, you've already written your Cross Markets into it. Just take a look at your manuscript. Where are the new markets?

• Does your main character love to cook? If so, no matter what kind of book you've written, cooking supply stores, cooking clubs, cooking schools, cooking tools websites and anything cooking related are great new cross markets!

• Does your main character live in a specific, historic or destination part of the world? Now you can cross market to the museums, welcome centers, gift shops and travel websites for that location.

• Does your main character travel, eat donuts, love chocolate, live on the beach or in the mountains?

PIZZA

Check out these examples of global pizza cross marketing:

Around the world, pizza toppings vary greatly, reflecting regional tastes and preferences. In Japan, for instance, eel and squid are favorites. In Pakistan, curry is a big seller. In Russia, red herring is the topping of choice. Australians enjoy shrimp and pineapple as well as barbeque toppings on their pies. Costa Ricans favor coconut.

~ Source: Numero Uno Pizzeria

Some of the more popular international toppings are pickled ginger, minced mutton and tofu in India; squid and Mayo Jaga (mayonnaise, potato and bacon) in Japan; and green peas in Brazil. In Russia, they serve pizza covered with mockba; a combination of sardines, tuna, mackerel, salmon and onions. In France, a popular combo is called the Flambé with bacon, onion, and fresh cream.

~ Source: Domino's Pizza

Have I made my point? The sublime magic of cross marketing is to go places other authors don't bother to go to reach readers. If your character loves coffee, there's no reason you can't ask coffee shops to permit you to post a daily comment on their website to promote your book. Each day you can mention the daily brew and if your werewolf private eye likes it, or which pie he prefers, or even what newspaper he's reading while enjoying his coffee.

Good cross marketing is about seeing beyond the average. Dig deep into your manuscript and find those possible markets. They're yours for the plucking simply because there is no competition with other books or the product you're connecting with. As long as the coffee store continues to gain customers, they're happy. And if you gain book buyers, everybody is happy!

ASSIGNMENT: Cross Marketing Magic

Finding the "Sublime" avenue for cross marketing requires forgetting everything you ever thought was standard for marketing a book. All those little tricks and things and audiences your author friends have suggested can't hold a candle to working with the "Sublime". So, how does one find the "Sublime"?

It's in the book you wrote and nowhere else. Think of every character, plot event, element, location and emotion in your book and make a list. A LONG list. Here's one for an imaginary book entitled Light on Light. For this exercise, we don't need to know the genre of the book or even the 10 – 15 word sound bite. All we need are words.

- *Northeastern Coast, Maine*
- *Winter, icy rain*
- *Storms keeps townspeople shut tight and warm inside*
- *Light Houses (three in area, one supposedly haunted)*
- *Blind children at boarding school for blind*
- *Spirituality, good and evil*
- *Hundreds of braille books stolen from the school*
- *Cookies made to raise money*
- *Evil Wicca, dark magic*
- *Grungy teen heroine: Markie, (Main Character - MC)*
- *MC is homeless and lives in haunted lighthouse (Ghosts don't bother her)*
- *MC loves lemonade, even in winter*
- *MC loves head banging rock and roll*
- *MC has a tattoo of an angel on her shoulder*
- *MC suspects she won't live to see 20 so she's a real risk taker*
- *MC wears a silver-coated wolf's fang around her neck*

Keep it going, make the list as long as possible. Now find your cross markets inside this list. Can this book sell well in Main tourist towns? Is it worth the cost to sell necklaces similar to the one Markie wore in the book? How about temporary, rub on tattoos like Markie's? Can you cross market to magic stores? In Lighthouse gift shops? Is it feasible to have a braille version of the book made available? How about cookies? Do those offer a cross market? Can you promote your book through bakeries or on bakery websites? If nothing else, can you do a whole promotion around the cookie recipe? Find the missing secret ingredient? Having such a unique, young heroine, can you cross market by making her the focus of your website? Or have her do her own blog? Maybe she can be the focus of a winter-time novella of "stay warm" stories?

With the right kind of sublime list in hand, sublime cross markets will shout right at you!

TURBO CREATIVE THINKING

How creative do you really think? As writers, we are free thinkers and do our best not to focus on the rules while we create, but those rules are there, looming even bigger if we're just getting started as an author. If you're attempting to gain a literary agent, there are all the query rules, format rules and acceptable approaches rules to consider. There are the rules about clean genre, clean manuscripts, clean elevator pitches. If we're going the independent or small publisher route, they have their own set of requirements and each one is different. If you self-publish, there are critical editing necessities, a formatting learning curve and of course, all the distribution and promotional systems to master.

With all these rules floating around, crowding and confusing the process from point A: the finished, beautifully imaginative novel you wrote, to point Z: the actual book sales, how creative can one really be? It's as though the course of action we must take simply chokes the creativity out of us. There are so many tiny commandments to follow it's too easy to get side-tracked into pleasing the process and forgetting the book buyer.

Let's break those patterns we learned in nursery school. Don't follow the rules. Don't worry about being correct. Don't question the process I'm about to suggest because if you do, you may find yourself spending more time satisfying the "system" and never reach your own goals.

Yes, sorry; I am from the sixties. It's time for a little REVOLUTION in the marketing process. It's time to tap into all the beautiful colors and emotions and excitement you felt while writing your book. Because frankly, if you don't recapture and convey that intensity, why should anyone want to buy your book?

See, it's not always just the perfect crafting of a 10 word sound bite or 25 word elevator pitch that gets someone's attention, it's the author's energy. That flash of enthusiasm can and should be in those few words, but it also must be present in the process the author uses to communicate with the prospective buyer.

It's time for a little mind-blowing magical mystery tour. Yes, this will seem weird for anyone born after 1975 but it will be fun. I'm going to ask you to take ten minutes out of your crazy day to just sit and clear your thoughts. Come on, you can spare a few minutes away from Twitter, Facebook, your iPhone and texting. This is important and it's most important you do it AWAY from your technology. Go outside and sit in the grass if you can. I know it sounds stupid but really, when your book idea came to you, what did you do? Get onto Twitter and Facebook? Text the world that you have an idea? My bet is that you didn't even sit at your keyboard right away. You sat someplace quiet and you thought. I need you to get back to that emotional space. Be peaceful. Clear everything else from your mind. Breathe evenly, meditate for a few moments if you can. Now that you're there, you can start.

Recall the process of evolving your story, how it came to you, all the curves and u-turns it took before it became the final novel. Feel the characters, what you like and don't like about each one, explore the emotions in the events in the book and then plant yourself firmly into the locations. Even if your book is fantasy, science fiction or deep historic, get yourself there, feel it, smell it, taste it. No grumbling. If you went this route to develop your story, it's not new to you. If you love your story, it's no hardship. Most importantly, if you reconnect this way, everything about marketing and cross marketing the wonderful book you wrote will be that much closer to you. So get into this. I promise, it will be rewarding.

Now come back from your journey slowly so that you can retain the magic you originally found in the story. Examine what you brought back with you. While still sitting quietly, jot down the biggest impressions you got. Now set it aside and do the whole thing again for ten minutes the next day, and the next. Do this for four or five days then collect your jotted notes and begin.

If your goal is to seriously attack and gain visibility and sales for your book, this process may seem a little bohemian, but just go with me here.

Start with the biggest impression. Perhaps it was "Green". Maybe your book is about ecology, or raising milk cows, or a romance about a playground planner falling for a beautiful politician who hates kids, but "Green" was the impression you wrote down. The key word is "Green". If "Green" stuck with you, it will stick with readers, but the goal is to get MORE readers than the average marketing strategy will reach. Let's play a mind stretching game and find a few cross markets. How many people can you capture with "Green"?

- Green – plants, the color, ecological organizations, paint stores, interior decorators
- Park – city parks, town parks, park developers, art parks, car parks, antique car clubs
- Farm – dairy farm, farm markets, vineyards, wine gift stores, wine tasting gatherings
- Garden – gardening clubs, online gardening groups, florists, flower arranging schools
- Herbs – cooking, chefs, culinary schools, cooking gadget stores, cookbook clubs
- Trees – bonsai, pine, oak, poplar, tree lined streets, tree of life
- Forest – forestry groups, camping groups, Robin Hood, survival groups
- Mountain – camping, hiking, rafting, skiing, climbing, wildlife preservation
- Money – teaching, becoming the expert, cross marketing, making BIG sales

That last one is me, getting you back to practicality but first let's talk about the other ideas. As you can see, some of these directions went way off track, but did they? Can they possibly work for the book at hand? The idea is not to think logically, but to let a concept like "Green" flow into as many different directions as you can find. Play with this. Laugh at it. Enjoy this process because that's a big part of regaining your joy for the book you wrote.

Getting back to heightened sensations recovered from the creative process for writing your book is the only, I repeat, ONLY road to being creative with marketing and cross marketing for your book. Using strategies and tried-and-true systems are good, but combine them with TURBO creative thinking is a powerful key to cross marketing success.

Now, of the ideas above, if the book is the romance about a playground planner falling for a beautiful politician who hates kids, let's see how many of the impressions and ideas above could work. Aside from the standard romance avenues for marketing, you can now cross market to:

- Playground designers associations
- Safe and ecological playground and park organizations
- City, county and local community center book stores
- Vineyards and wine gift stores (for the romance aspect)
- Gardening clubs
- Romantic cookbook stores or cooking classes

You can speak about safe playgrounds or ecology, or cooking for children or making romance part of everyday life or including kids in helping in the garden or kitchen – in other words, you can become the expert on these subjects and speak to a variety of audiences.

Not one of these ideas fall into the standard romance marketing category because now you're thinking about Cross Marketing, and thinking about it in a productive way!

All right, you can put away your bellbottoms, tie-dyed tee shirt and headband now.

EXPAND YOUR PLATFORMS

I know what you're thinking. Your mind is spinning with all the activity you've already created for your various platforms. You have a large following on Twitter and make sure you interact every day. You've built your friend base on Facebook to the max. You blog, you email, you interact with other authors. What else could you possibly do? And how much time will it take? You're a writer, at some point you would like to be writing, right?

Take a deep breath and relax, this isn't what you think. Yes, you have done as much as you can with your websites, social marketing and group affiliations, but have you? Are your efforts gaining the responses and results you want? Are you talking to the right people, the BOOK BUYING people? Relax. You are doing well, but it's time to talk about how to help you do better with cross marketing.

Have you ever heard the phrase "make money with somebody else's money"? Well, it sounds a little tacky and distasteful, but sometimes you need to look into another platformer's back yard to find a few more book buyers. No, I'm not talking about stealing friends or followers from other authors. In fact, far from it. I'm talking about strolling through an entirely different neighborhood to find more book buyers.

Here are the facts. Most authors feel safer making friends and followers with other authors. It's a great resource for information and great support as you plot or develop characters. It's a fantastic group of people for input on your book cover ideas and gaining insight into your agent, publisher, format or distribution choices. But the truth is that authors don't buy other authors books, at least not enough to make a major impact on your sales. In reality, all of your author friends have already paid the price in time, advice and kindness while you showed them version after version of your book video or healed from your rejection wounds. If I bought a book from every author I've friended on social media, I'd have thousands of books! It simply doesn't make sense to put too much hope into selling books to other authors.

So, now that over three-quarters of your Twitter and Facebook followers are authors and writers, where do you look for book buyers? This is where the Cross Marketing magic really happens.

As I've mentioned a number of times over the years, everything you need to be successful with your book sales in INSIDE your manuscript. I recently heard a comment from a student at one of my workshops who doubted that cross marketing could never work with her genre – erotica. This is how it can work with EVERY genre.

To start this thinking process, I'm going to choose a genre and story plot point that is fairly simple. Let's say your book is a murder mystery about a woman who owns an auto repair business and loves to be under the hood, dirty and greasy. How the murder is discovered or solved isn't relevant for this exercise, so let's just go with what we have.

Let's say you've already promoted it to all your Facebook friends and followers (many of whom are other writers and authors). Now what do you do?

Expanding platforms through Cross Marketing is about taking advantage of someone else's platforms. In the best case scenario, someone whose platform audience will find no conflict of interest and - most important - the platform owner has no competition should you sell a book to their customers.

Back to our auto mechanic. Here are a few platforms the author could take advantage of.

Book Clubs
- Not just the obvious mystery readers book clubs, but how about "How to" book clubs? How about car or machinery lovers book clubs?

Group Affiliations
- Car lovers groups
- Car maintenance groups
- How to change your oil/sparkplugs/tires groups for women

Live Local Business Connections (never discount readers just outside your own door)
- Pop by every oil change or auto services business and post a flyer or business card about your book on the bulletin board
- Do the same with every auto parts supply store
- Join the Chamber of Commerce and make "friendly" contacts for more ideas
- Give away a free book at an antique car club gathering, or sell books there along with some free lemonade

Website Connections
- Local and national auto service businesses (independent and chains) all have websites. Take a good look at those websites, find the contact and find out if you can post at their website, perhaps a photo of your book cover, or better yet, a daily "Mechanical Murder" tip that talks about auto service and solving murders. If you can create a following on two or three of those major websites, your sales will jump!
- How about asking to do this on Auto Clubs (like AAA) websites?

Blogs and Yahoo Groups
- How many blogs exist that discuss women and auto repairs? Women who are mechanically helpless? Women who are mechanically savvy? Find them and ask to be a guest blogger to promote your book and do the guest blogs in a series so you can spread out the exposure.
- Seek out Yahoo Groups that cover all the angles in your book, women, women mechanics, murder mystery lovers. Join, make friends and make sure your email promo tag for the book is prominent with every response you make to the group.

All right, back to the question of an erotica writer doing some cross marketing. Granted, mainstream situations may be out of the question for a hard erotica book, but there are many other cross marketing opportunities most erotica writers haven't actually explored.

Check into website connections, for example, can you get your book promoted on a sex toy or sexy lingerie website? Perhaps you can become part of one of their forums and chat away about your book to a new audience you haven't reached so far. If your book is paranormal in nature, it's not outside the box to connect with Paranormal Romance Yahoo groups, Facebook Groups or Twitter fans. Take your time, explore every avenue. Can you make yourself an expert in something the erotica community is interested in? If so, go for it. Cross marketing isn't something you can't use because it approaches a broad audience, it's something you NEED to use because in any tight genre, expanding the interest base and attracting more and new buyers for your books is all that matters. Cross marketing for erotica needs to work within its own universe, just like cozy romance or children's books. It's all about looking for your prospective book buyers where you haven't looked before, and connecting with them.

Once an author has EXPANDED their platforms with cross marketing, the whole world opens up for building a bigger fan base, stronger sales and greater demand for more books!

"Conformity is the jailer of freedom and the enemy of growth."

~ John F. Kennedy

LOCATING YOUR ALTERNATIVE MARKETS

Where do you find readers for your book? How to you search for them and how can you know which avenue will be successful and which will be a bust?

Imagine you're in a different city and have to go to the grocery store. As similar and organized as grocery stores across the country can be, you simply can't find the product you're looking for. Perhaps you want a pound of coffee. Usually it's on the shelves with tea and dry coffee creamers, but in this store, you just can't locate it. Where would you look? With the baking goods? The cake mixes and sugar? Perhaps it's in the aisle with the cookies and packaged cakes? Maybe it's with the cereals and dry breakfast items. Could it be with the breads? Maybe this particular store has a special aisle just for hot coffee beverages, specialty imported coffees, hot chocolate mixes and flavored coffees? Still can't find it, perhaps you should try the bakery section of the store, they may have set up a coffee display along the beautiful fresh baked goods there.

In other words, where might you find the coffee? If you think hard enough, you can probably determine ten or fifteen fairly logical places for the store to stock their coffee cans.

It's the same with your book. Just because it's a "pound of coffee" doesn't mean there's only one place to display it. If you dissect your manuscript, you will find several different possible places to find your prospective book buyer/reader/fan. Trust me, this works.

To find alternative markets for your book, you must revisit EVERYTHING in your book. Make a list of every possible alternative reader you can think of then go in for deeper exploration.

For example, let's try this with a random book.

- Genre – Murder Mystery/Historic
- Location – Eastern seaside town, 1910
- Event 1 – The murder takes place in a lighthouse
- Event 2 – The town suspects an elderly man of the murder
- Character 1 preferences – Detective chews black licorice and smokes cigars

- Character 2 preferences – His wife, the protagonist who has an instinct that the elderly man is innocent, is a gardener who discovers the murder weapon in her own petunia patch
- Standard interest groups – Mystery lovers and mystery book clubs. Historic lovers and historic book clubs.
- Cross marketing groups – Lighthouse lovers, tourist websites to lighthouses and seaside locations. Cigar websites. Licorice and candy websites, gardening groups and gardening supply websites.
- Online exposure – Create a Facebook page just for the book and connect with the groups listed above. Contact the websites listed above and either become active in their discussions or ask to post your book on their websites. Do the same with lighthouse, cigar and gardening bloggers. Build a book website for your book and develop a page specifically to attract lighthouse lovers. Create a blog just for lighthouse or cigar lovers or garden lovers and build new fans there by promoting your book after each entry.
- Publicity angle – Historic lighthouses need funding support for maintenance
- Media – After deciding to create a fundraiser or participate in a fundraiser to support historic lighthouses, standard press releases to all eastern seaside town papers and magazines.

All right, this is a great list, but is it reasonable? Perhaps your detective character really does love cigars, but you know nothing about cigars. Perhaps cigars, attracting mostly a male buyer, would be the wrong audience to go after for your book which is written to attract mostly female readers. What if, of all things, the licorice direction can prove very lucrative? Maybe you located a specialty licorice company with a really cool website and they're thrilled to have your book featured there. Look what you've got! You get to sell books to new readers and there's no competition between you and the candy maker.

Now, take a serious look at the lighthouse element. The power of this particular approach is that all along the eastern and western seaboard, and the great lakes are lighthouses. These structures have been a fascination for over a century to many, many people. There are huge organizations of lighthouse lovers who dedicate their time and money to visiting, climbing and supporting the maintenance of lighthouses. This is an extremely good direction to go. Getting involved with a fundraiser for these organizations on a local or even national level can only help expose your book in a big way to a big new readership.

Online, you'll need to really play with your cross markets. Don't just join a Yahoo lighthouse lovers group and announce that you've written a book, get involved with the group. Chat. Make friends. Always have your email tag visible and let it do the selling for you. In groups like that, people buy from friends, not interlopers who pop in, talk about themselves and their book then leave. Make sure your Author and Book websites are active with lots of interesting information so that possible book buyers come back regularly to see what's new. Regarding a blog, yes, you want a book blog, but be sure to create a blog category about lighthouses because this can do something magical for you – it can establish you as an expert of sorts.

The goal is to help you locate your possible cross markets. Dig deep into your manuscript and make your own list like the one above. Let yourself go wild with it, you never know where there might be a fantastic hidden alternative market you never thought about before. After you've developed the list, bring a critical eye to it. What will not work? What markets are simply too time consuming and difficult to approach? What seems like a simple market to approach? What feels right and what feels wrong? You know your book intimately and only you can dissect it and find the cross marketing gems inside.

HOW TO APPROACH CROSS MARKETS

We've explored various ways of locating possible cross markets and now we're going to talk about approaching the markets you've uncovered.

After you've explored all the possible cross markets for your book based on genre, subgenre and unique elements inside the manuscript (locations, character likes and dislikes, sub-plots), you have now identified a few new groups of possible markets. Go through them carefully, perhaps test them in a small way before moving on to the next step. For example, if your book is a murder mystery and you're seeking book clubs to promote and gain reviews through, you may want to look closely. What if that particular book club is partial to cozy, Christian or YA mysteries? You must know this, because if your book uses colorful language or includes a sex scene or two, you have just barked up the wrong tree and it can become very ugly. The last thing you want is someone saying something negative about your book or your tactics for marketing it. Know your genres and markets very clearly before you do anything. Mistakes like the one above can hurt you down the road because people know people, and if you write another book in another genre and your name is a little tarnished, it might not go well for you.

Cross marketing can be risky business but only if you're not paying attention to the details. If you're approaching gardening groups for your romance, make sure your book has enough gardening in it to be of interest to the group. Be careful about hard selling to romance groups too. Many urban fantasies, mysteries, even horror and adventure books have some romantic elements in them, but be sure they have enough to qualify – in other words, a quick sexual encounter is not a romance to most readers. A love story twisted into a murder adventure just might qualify. Be careful how you use genre, readers aren't stupid and they know a romance when they see one. A sultry look and dirty thought depicted in the third paragraph on page four does not qualify.

Genres

Genres have been strict for many reasons but you need to only be careful of the primary direction you want to go with your Cross Marketing. Using genre means stretching it as far as is rational. Never go too far. A horror adventure about zombies dying and decaying in a field will not qualify as a great read for a group of ecological earth renewal advocates. Be practical. Of course, if your main character, the hero who saves the world, is an earth renewal and sustainability expert, you may have something there. Always be honest about the primary genre. If you're afraid to tell a group that the book is really about zombies, it may be the wrong group. Choose carefully what cross markets are best suited for your book.

Smile and Make Nice

Approaching qualified cross markets is a touchy feely thing. First of all, I don't suggest that you approach more than one cross market at a time. It takes full attention to understand all the nuances of that new market and if you pound away at three or four, you might lose some focus as well as miss a few opportunities you didn't see coming. For example, if you are planning to approach coffee shop websites in hopes of promoting your book because your main character is an avid coffee lover, AND you approach mystery lovers book clubs because the sub-plot of your book has a mystery in it, AND you want to approach several paranormal clubs and groups because a portion of your book explores ghost interaction and paranormal events, it's too much to go for at once. Choose one to start with, preferably the most promising target. Let's say the paranormal groups is your first approach because the ghost and paranormal activity is a) in at least two thirds of your book and b) has the strongest interest target, as confirmed by the number of followers on Twitter or Facebook for paranormal and ghost related accounts. After you've seen activity and qualify that this cross marketing direction is a positive one, make it a stable daily activity then move on to the next.

Interest Groups

After you join a group, you must make friends, get involved and participate. Yes, yes, I know that inside your mind all you're thinking is "get sales!" but this just doesn't work that way. Every time you connect with one of these cross market groups, it should be in response to someone else's post. Insert yourself into conversations and become a contributor within those conversations. Make sure you have your book clearly in the tag line of every response you make. After a few days you'll have a good idea of how this particular group works and what their primary interests are. If it doesn't suit you, quietly bow out. If it does, begin a subject of your own and no, it can't be that you wrote a book. You've joined a group focused on a subject that interests you or it wouldn't be in your book, so talk about that subject and make sure to leave an open ended question at the end of your post to invite responses.

Now, let's say you've gotten one new cross market rocking, if it's paranormal online groups, perhaps now you can begin gaining Twitter followers and Facebook friends from these kinds of interest groups. Approach each person and group the same way, smile, introduce yourself, make friends, get involved and make sure there's a tag about your book everywhere. Now, if someone asks about that book, you've gotten an invitation to pitch away!

Non-Competitive Businesses

The next target cross market you may want to approach is the websites. Business and interest websites are a little different, and the most effective ones are the ones that have no competition. For example, of your book is a paranormal romance and you get involved with every paranormal fiction and supernatural story website around, you will have some serious competition. Trust me, every other paranormal author on the planet has thought to approach them. You're plan is to do something far more effective.

Let's talk about the main character who loves coffee. Coffee websites sell coffee. If you manage to sell a few books by being affiliated with their website, they have no issues because you are not taking sales from them. Research these websites, how many are there? What do they look like? Do they have a large following or small following? You can tell by how active the website is. If they don't update daily or weekly, you don't want them. But if they're active, this is where the magic starts! You will need to approach the owners of these websites. Simply contact them and ask if you, the author of a murder mystery where the main character loves coffee, can participate in their website. They may permit you to purchase or place an ad for your book (passive, and not always the best option), or they may welcome you as a guest blogger (a great opportunity to not only get your name out, but also the name of your character and book) or perhaps they'll let you create a daily or weekly feature on their website, like "Detective Moore's coffee grind of the day." You can choose a specific coffee the website sells or lists and do a little daily tip from the good "detective" to the website visitors.

Once you get permission, don't dilly-dally. Move on it right away. Don't miss a beat, a day or a week. Be constant with your efforts and you will gain sales, you'll be amazed. If the company will only allow you an ad and it's at a reasonable price, do it, and make sure something in your ad states that "Coffee and Detective Moore are the perfect afternoon reading mix!"

Move on to the next coffee website and start again. At any given time, you may be present on as many as five or six different coffee websites! Here's the trick – no two websites are receiving the same thing. In other words, if you're doing a daily coffee tip from the good detective on coffee website A, have placed an ad on coffee website B, then you need to do something different on coffee website C, D, etc. You can post excerpts from your book. You can run a contest to win a free copy of your book. You can create clues and do your own mystery on one of those websites – run by Detective Moore, of course.

I strongly suggest you keep a chart so you can keep track of these activities. It's good for your time management, and it's good for tracking success or failure.

Charities

The last category I'd like to discuss is charities. This only works if your book touches on or relates to a subject that will work as a public relations direction – i.e. your main character is fighting to save the rainforest, or help save a young girl suffering from cancer, or dealing with the plight of baby seals at the North Pole. These are important and wonderful directions in which to cross market, especially if you're donating a portion of the sales of your book to that charity.

You can take this further. You can create fundraisers for the charity through your book, you can become a part of other events and make it always known that a portion of the book sales go to a particular charity, and you can ask to participate in that charities' website much the same way you do above, in the non-competitive business section.

Remember, to do this you must seriously contact and discuss it with someone at the charity. They have rules, they have paperwork, they have procedures and they have specific logo images you can and cannot use.

Cross marketing through a charity is a perfect way to create a new audience. Many will purchase the book simply because it helps a cause they care about. Those people are readers and they have friends who are readers and all these readers would have never been reached through the standard genre pitch form of marketing.

Now you have it. The approach to each cross market must be done carefully and with a gentle hand. You're stepping into an arena that isn't about hard sell, talking to a collection of prospective book buyers who aren't currently thinking about books, and cultivating a new market where, in most cases, no author has gone before. Fear not.

"One often meets his destiny on the road he takes to avoid it."

~ Oogway from the DreamWorks Animation film, Kung Fu Panda

HOW TO MAINTAIN CROSS MARKETS

Marketing a book today is a major undertaking and almost every ounce of that work falls on the author's shoulders. With a good Book Business Plan, a powerful set of Platforms, elegant marketing, publicity and promotion you can go far, but only so far. Cross marketing is the key to breaking into big sales because it works in tandem with your manuscript, making the efforts unique to you and your book. And it approaches markets other typical genre authors don't think to approach. Sales success is all in the author's hands and only you can determine to take that extra step into the unknown to garner numbers that set you and your book apart.

No one said this would be easy, but I've told you often that it is simple.

So now you've found new cross markets and approached them. Let's say you've been successful with some of these cross markets and you don't want the success to stop. There are techniques to maintain and grow awareness within cross markets. Let's break this down and follow the same categories we used to help with the discovery of and approach to new markets for your book.

Genres

Here you may be a little limited, especially if your genre is extremely specific – like children's books, religious or hard erotica – but in most cases you can grow within the new subgenre for as long as the readers will have you. If you've written a mystery with heavy romantic undertones and at least one paranormal element, you could be golden. You can be selling your book to mystery lovers, romance readers and paranormal book junkies. That's three audiences instead of one. The question is, how do you keep the love growing? This takes some careful strategies.

<u>Gain reviews from reputable reviewers in those genres</u> – Of course you want good, strong reviews from mystery reviewers because it's your primary genre, but one thing you need to do is get good strong reviews from romance and paranormal reviewers too. Those reviewers have large audiences within the genre and can, with the post of one review, gain substantial sales for you. Seek out as many reviewers as possible within all your cross market genres and be sure to clearly state that your book has strong storylines within the genres the reviewers are working with. Never just assume the reviewer will understand that your book entitled Murder in the Tropics has paranormal or romantic elements, tell them. Don't be afraid to give away parts of your story. Spoilers are one thing, but imagining that a reviewer will search for the element that interests them is foolish and a sure way to end up in the trash/recycle bin.

<u>Promote those reviews to a larger audience of that subgenre</u> – When you get a great review in one of your cross market subgenres, don't just automatically promote it to your regular followers and expect a huge sales jump, those folks have already heard the story. Talking to the same people over and over will not gain new sales. You must take it outside the normal venues. Make your announcements to paranormal and romance groups. Those are the places to promote the great review for your book.

Seek out new venues to reach more variables within that subgenre – Don't stop with the obvious. Romance groups love romance, but who else loves romance? Nurses? Dentists? School teachers? Housewives? Mothers? How can you approach them? The odds are smaller but they are still sales! If one nurse loved the book and mentions it to another and another, well, it can grow! If it ends there, it's three more sales than you originally had and a tested cross market. Who likes paranormal? Would they like the paranormal elements in your book? One way to seek those people out is by searching "paranormal" on Twitter or Facebook and seeing what comes up. 10 people? 10,000 people? Are they worth approaching? Your choice. Me? I'll shoot for those 10 or 10,000 more book sales. How do you find these groups in the live world? Just look around. Most organizations, no matter what they specialize in, are always looking for speakers for interesting, social and creative subjects for their meetings. Talk to the library, how many different kinds of groups meet there? Look into social halls and organizations, women's clubs, ski clubs. You will find groups looking for something stimulating to feature at an upcoming meeting. Why can't it be your fantastic book?

Sociability

Remember the "Smile and Make Nice" information earlier? Well now I'm going to ask you to make even nicer. Be an online and alive social butterfly. I want to see your name everywhere. When was the last time you Googled yourself? Try it now and be amazed. Is there one page of you? Ten? Twenty? Are they all related to the book(s) you want to sell? The reviews you want people to notice? The news about your book? If not, your efforts may be too scattered.

Try this, every time you use your name, make sure you use the name of your book and the 10 word soundbite/tag for your book. Making these connections in interviews, blogs, tweets and Facebook entries can create a substantial synergy between you, your book and your various audiences.

Take a moment to introduce yourself to cross market groups and segments by immediately connecting you with your book. It can be as subtle as making sure the tag is on every single email you send out, or it can be as elaborate as offering a free book to the person who responds to your introduction with the most interesting Mystery (or Romance or Paranormal) comment. Making friends is nice, making strong friends in a big way is power.

Interest Groups

You may have approached reading groups and book clubs, you may have approached other groups specific to the elements in your book – coffee lovers, gardeners, flying fanatics, etc. But after you give your first approach and see a little sales growth, you can't just sit and hope it continues. These groups are collections of people, and people only like, trust and purchase from other likeable, trustworthy people. When I told you to "make friends" in these groups and keep the sales pitch to a minimum, I mean to seriously make friends with these groups. That means getting involved. If the group is doing a fundraiser, offer help either in time, contacts or a free book or two for the silent auction. If the group is planning a live get-together in New Orleans, try to get there if you can. Trust me, face-to-face has far more impact than online connections. You may make friends for life in the Crescent City who will wholeheartedly and tirelessly promote your book just because they like you so much in person. (Talk about a Big Easy!)

If the group needs ideas for a project, chime in. If they need an answer you can help with, offer it. Remember, these are your friends now and they want to help you too. Wouldn't it be fantastic to use them for research for your next book? They'll be thrilled to help because you've been so much help to them. They'll tell their friends in other groups about you and your book.

Going the distance with interest groups is a real win/win, but only if you do it with the future in mind. If you approach the group and think only of what sales you can gain quickly then disappear, there's little chance of your popping back in for your next book and getting a favorable response. Play nice and they'll play nice right back.

Non-competitive Businesses

Serious cross marketing is about digging deeper than you think. Yes, you've done some wonderful things with connecting your book with coffee shop websites because your main character loves coffee, but have you gone far enough? Here are a few suggestions that might spur new ideas:

- Coffee recipe websites
- Coffee Mug websites
- Contests on various websites where you give away a copy of your book and the coffee company also gives away something – a coupon for a free cup of joe or a discount on a pound of coffee. Or maybe have people create a coffee drink (alcoholic or not) and win a free book
- Coffee Tasting/Book Signing parties, or how about creating a Coffee and Book PAIRING group of your own?
- Coffee/Tea lovers groups, websites and groups
- Develop "TeaTeasers" or "CoffeeBeans", small hints about your story that can entice tea or coffee lovers at a website or tea store into reading your book.
- Write a weekly blog or column for a coffee blog or publication – the by-line will be your coffee loving character, of course.

And all of this is just from one concept – coffee. Let your imagination travel. What is one of your specific Cross Markets and how many different ways can you think of to grow it deeper and wider?

Charities

There are a few strong theories on working with charities. Some say you can spread yourself around and support several charities, others feel the loyalty focus is more effective for you and your charity of choice. Honestly, it is your decision to make.

Personally, I've always felt that choosing a charity is an important part of defining who you are as an author. If you wish to support a charity, it should have a personal connection or a strong social affiliation you really want to be connected to on a variety of levels. Choosing a charity just because it might gain visibility is foolish and basically, unproductive. It's like you ooze some kind of stink that tells everyone you're just doing it for yourself. We all know what it means to support a charity and mean it. I strongly suggest you do that.

Assuming you chose the charity because it somehow fits with your story, or at least the point of your story, you can do more than just announce that you support that group. There are several ways to support your charity and to explain it, I'll take my charity of choice. For this book, these are some of the activities I plan to do in support of my chosen charity, The American Literacy Council.

- Donate a portion of book sales profits to The American Literacy Council
- Speak at various colleges, universities and high schools about the techniques in the book, and the challenges of The American Literacy Council
- Set a goal and make it known on my author and book website that I wish to raise X amount of dollars for The American Literacy Council
- Offer assistance when The American Literacy Council is doing a fund raising event in my area
- Ask to be part of The American Literacy Council's newsletter or blog, possibly with a monthly blog or brief column on literacy and fiction in America
- Purchase ads for my book in church bulletins, school newsletters, online websites for colleges and universities, all with a tag that a portion of the profits for book sales go to the American Literacy Council.

As you can see, there's more to it than just noting on the last page or back cover of your book that you are supporting a charity with the sales of the book. You must get involved, become known and connected with the charity.

Charities can be the most powerful tool in your cross marketing arsenal. Use it wisely and with gusto.

"I am not interested in preserving the status quo. I am interested in overthrowing it."
~ Niccolo Machiavelli
Italian writer and statesman, Florentine patriot, 1469 - 1527

CROSS MARKETING WORKSHEET

Every element of your cross marketing strategy should be documented and tested. It's not good enough to try something and discover a few weeks later "Oh wow! That really worked! Now, what was it I did, exactly?" To build momentum for your book's visibility, interest and sales you need to know what you're attempting, what your goals are, and you must clearly document how successful or unsuccessful each effort is.

If you think a specific cross market is perfect for your book and you try it, how do you really know if it was successful or not? In your head, it might seem like a perfect fit, but did it really work? Of course, you will be running at least two or three different cross market approaches at the same time, plus your standard marketing to the obvious target markets, but how can you break it down to see which effort was successful and which was not so successful? How much success makes a cross market direction worthy of additional exploration?

There are a few critical red flags involved here, and among them are the biggest three that torment most authors.

Hope – We hope that people like our book and just wish for great results. We're looking for emotional, professional, personal and maybe even spiritual validation, a reason to go on. Okay, maybe that's a little too dramatic but you get my point. I call Hope a non-strategy. It falls under the category of inaction and must always be checked at the door when testing your marketing and especially your cross marketing, because there's easily twice as much of a chance for criticism in an unsuspecting, ill-approached cross market as there will be in the normal genre market strategy.

Imagined Credibility – This one doesn't only apply to cross marketing, it applies to writing your book in the first place. Words you might say to yourself under the influence of imagined credibility are: Oh, people will love this idea! People need to read more books like this. (And my favorite) If I just explain my reasoning they'll buy my book by the millions! Trust me, if you have to explain anything to anyone, it's not working, whether we're talking about your plot or your cross marketing strategy. Simplicity is what attracts people, and reality is what attracts cross markets. If you think that gardening clubs will love your book because your main character has a back yard garden, you may be way off base. Be credible with your cross marketing. It will take a lot of focus on that character's garden to attract the attention of gardening clubs and groups. That garden must almost be a main character. If it isn't, this would be like approaching dentist groups because one of your main character brushes his teeth once in the book. Imagined credibility is another non-strategy.

Fear – This one can put a real kibosh on your plans, no matter how well thought out and possibly successful your cross marketing ideas are. Try to look on the bright side. What are you really afraid of? If a cross market does not respond to your efforts, there's nothing lost. It's not like your primary genre has stepped up and insisted you stink. It's an extra step for seeking new and more readers and the point of all this is to test uncharted waters. Face your fears, take a leap and see what happens. Fear is a non-strategy.

In all three of these cases – Hope, Imagined Credibility and Fear – you need to recognize them for what they are: non-strategies and ineffective wastes of time. I usually simply mark them "DUH" because, of course, I knew better when I implemented them in the first place.

So, how do you keep track of all this Cross Market activity? You must create a worksheet that:

- Develops creative exploration for Cross Markets
- Establishes a testing system to determine if the Cross Market is viable and
- Expands on good ideas while eliminating the bad ideas.

You must set standards. Creating a worksheet to help you navigate through the process can be a simple plan or a complex plan. It can be created on spreadsheet forms or on a yellow lined pad. There are three primary tasks listed above and three non-strategy situations to avoid.

Because marketing and cross marketing your book is such a personal thing, I strongly encourage you to create your own worksheet, but to help you visualize, I've suggested a sample cross marketing worksheet as an assignment.

Remember, every book and every author is different, so make sure your worksheet is specific to your book, your genre, your subgenres and your sensibilities. Make the plan aggressive enough but also not too large to manage effectively. Activity is the key to success and remember, you must put in the work.

This is just a sample worksheet designed to help you avoid wasting time on non-strategies and track your Cross Marketing strategies for success. The way I use this it to print out several copies of a sheet with nothing but the titles and categories, then I just hand write my observations at the end of every week. I stack these sheets one over the other so that at the end of a month, I have four reports to review.

SAMPLE CROSS MARKETING WORKSHEET

Book Title	Callie's Spirit
25 Word Synopsis	Callie Cohen, small town seamstress, has an extraordinary client from 150 years in the past who teaches her some powerful life and love lessons
Primary Genre	Women's Fiction
Primary Target	Women, 18 -60
Possible Subgenres	Paranormal, Paranormal (light) Romance, YA

OBVIOUS MARKETS

Target 1	Women's Fiction book clubs
Target 2	Fans of paranormal romance and YA
Target 3	All my author friends (DUH, non-strategy – Authors are not effective sales target)

SUBLIME CROSS MARKETS

Hidden target 1	Callie is a seamstress, possibly fashion fans would like book
Hidden target 2	The story takes place in the Outer Banks of S.C, possible local and tourist fans. Callie also spends a lot of time at lighthouses (there are several in the Outer Banks)
Hidden target 3	Historical story line might interest history buffs, historical followers of the area and/or historical book clubs
Hidden target 4	Supporters of the historic Lighthouses in the Outer Banks might be interested
Hidden target 5	Fashion Design students (DUH, non-strategy – Design students are more interested in learning to design than reading my book)
Hidden target 6	Sewing store customers

NOTE – Use the Turbo Creative Thinking process to develop as many Sublime Cross Markets as possible, then weed them out for practicality. Mark the DUH, non-strategy ideas but keep them visible on your worksheet so that you don't tend to move back into that direction.

PLATFORM STRATEGIES

Book website	Must be kept active to hold primary market interest and maintain newly acquired fans from Cross Markets. Have regular updates on characters, area points of interest, even harsh weather reports in that area or correlating historical events that relate to the book.
Blog	Write weekly blog covering the strongest theme of my book. Talk about history, the area, work as a seamstress 150 years ago and in contemporary times. Become the expert in these areas.
Social Media	Twitter, Facebook, etc. as author and as book. Create fan page for Callie's Spirit and target friends and followers of the genre, sub-genre and those interested in your book's subject and Cross Market themes.
Group Affiliations	Join Cross Market groups (i.e. lighthouse lovers groups, paranormal/ghost lovers groups, historical clothing groups). List them and remember to really join, not just show up and pitch my book. Share about my book's topics and gain insight from other group members.
Live Connections	This is important! Create connections with LIVE businesses and groups that have common interests in the topics in my book. They don't need to be book clubs, they can simply be historical clubs or sewing clubs or even seaside businesses. Would the local gift store like to carry my book? Would the local library be willing to shelf my book or permit me time to speak about my book? Would the local crafts and sewing store like to display my book? All good connections. List them and schedule time to talk with them.
Website Connections	List all the online Cross Market strategies. The sewing company website might love to display your book and buy link. Same with the paranormal research websites. Try approaching the historical websites and asking to post my book there. Remember to give something back. Some websites will charge for an "ad" others might love it if the author writes a brief blog occasionally that connects their site with my book.
Guest Blogging	Strategize with blogs that are talking to my Cross Markets and offer to do a guest blog – not a blog about my book, a blog about what interests the blog reader with a secondary note that I am the author of a book that features history or historic clothing or lighthouses or whatever subject is appropriate. NOTE: Never just use the same guest blog each time, Google is not big on repeated content, and each blog audience deserves a special approach.
Charities	Approach appropriate charities, for example lighthouses are always trying to raise money, there might be a fund for retired historians or seamstresses, I might want to develop support for paranormal investigators. Find the right, most powerful charity to connect with my book and either commit a portion of the book sales to that charity or create a fundraising event for it.

NOTE: Be sure to review lessons 6, 7 and 8 on Locating, Approaching and Maintaining your Cross Markets.

SCHEDULE

Cross Market 1	Fashion
Strategy	Try to post on fashion websites
Start Date	June 1
End Date	June 30
Test Tool	Offer free book contest to followers of that website
Evaluation	Non-effective, no sales and no one tried to win free book

Cross Market 2	Historic
Strategy	Historic book clubs, lighthouse blogs and gift shops, historic clothing shop websites
Start Date	June 1
End Date	June 30
Test Tool	Interaction from this Cross Market
Evaluation	Many comments on blogs, good reception from book clubs, some comments on posts at historic clothing shop websites and gift shops at lighthouses. Unclear on number of sales for this Cross Market, but worthy of continued effort

Cross Market 3	Charity – Raising funds for lighthouse upkeep
Strategy	Offering and gaining free promotions from charity, press campaign that book is raising funds for charity
Start Date	June 1
End Date	June 30
Test Tool	Sales through coded purchases (purchase only at one location or online book store for charity to receive funds)
Evaluation	Sales have shown very successful, continue for 6 more months.

NOTE: Try not to approach more than three cross markets at the same time and remember to keep your focus on your primary markets active.

Part 7

IN CLOSING

It's only a meatball. Just a list of ingredients you put together, mix, roll and cook. Planning your success strategy is nothing more than a recipe, a system. You determine your goals, develop approaches that make sense for you and your book then do the work. Hopefully along the way you make new friends and have some fun. You will make mistakes, a plan may crumble or run amuck but you know the drill. You've been there before, whether it had to do with choosing and changing your major in college or determining which car to buy or contractor to hire. It's a process. And if you look at this the same way you look at planning the week's menu for your family or putting together a wardrobe for work or vacation, it gets easier, I promise.

It's only a meatball and you can change the recipe any way you like. Add more Parmesan cheese or maybe change it to Romano cheese, use fennel and add hot sausage to the ground beef. More garlic? Less oregano? All up to you. It's not brain surgery, no one is going to die. The key to this is to keep trying formulas until you get exactly what you want for your plans. Making mistakes is good, tweaking your strategy is vital. This is a new world of publishing and looking at marketing, publicizing and promoting your own book is an exciting prospect. It puts your destiny and accomplishments all in your own hands and nothing feels better than that.

Never fear, be courageous and try something new. Just because no author has tried it before does not mean it won't work. And remember, what works for you may not work for another author, their book or genre. Break new ground and explore new territories. As long as you always keep your eyes on the prize and know your book and goals intimately, you can't go wrong. When an author is too fearful or too lazy to explore new options and chooses the tired old formulas, they get only as far as the old formulas can take them. You are better than that, you've already written a book no one else could write, so why would you use someone else's marketing strategies?

Tools for Focus

Most writers and authors I know are so much more. They are mothers and fathers, caregivers, homemakers, cooks and bread winners. They work day (or night) jobs as accountants, factory workers, cashiers, salespeople, business owners and top executives. They all struggle with finding the balance between their writing passion, their family and meeting their mortgage. Life is complicated enough without trying to write, but every one of them is driven, obsessed with their plots and characters, striving for perfection with the written word and usually dog tired. They're courageous and talented and among the most creative and busy people I know.

Now, add negotiating the shifting paradigm of the publishing industry and what do you get? A borderline crazy person. Some writers are new and baffled by the vacillating publishing maze. Some are embedded in the original publishing business model and having a difficult time accepting the reality of this new landscape.

I'm proposing that change is deceivingly simple, it's just our mindset that makes it appear complicated. Never panic.

Rising up from all this upheaval is more promise and potential than a writer ever had in history. There are more options and variations available than there were just a handful of years ago … and it continues to shift and grow! All avenues should be explored, dissected and considered. Traditional publishing, sprouting indie-publishers, self-publishing, POD, e-publishing, market shifts in reader genre preferences, purchasing outlets and how the reader likes to read a book. Yes, it seems like the zoo has gotten overpopulated, but really, the reader base has expanded vastly and that's a good thing.

Make Solid Plans

Don't shy away from making solid plans. It's no different than plotting your novel. All you're doing now is plotting your success. You need a Book Business Plan, Author and Book Platforms plans, a Social Networking plan, a Marketing Plan, a Promotions Plan, a Press Campaign Plan, a Speaking Engagement/Event/Book Signing Plan and a plan for writing your next book. Close your eyes and imagine the success you want, then simply get it all down on paper.

Be Gentle with Yourself

I do want to give you some good advice as you do all this … be gentle with yourself and your activities. Everything doesn't have to be done at once, in fact, everything shouldn't be done at once. Take one step at a time. Tackle things like Twitter or Facebook or blogging with enthusiasm, knowing every effort will pay off down the road. Perfect each element then add the next. Don't become overwhelmed or overworked. Look at this as a joy, as paving the way for book sales and gaining everything you want. Avoid frustrations by simply taking a moment, walking away from the computer and strolling down the street for some fresh air. Do some yoga. Go to the health club and work off the steam.

Arrange regular breaks from your work. Plan a monthly lunch with friends or family or other authors. Schedule a monthly online chat with friends far away. Take in a matinee. Step away and return refreshed.

Remember, your book didn't happen quickly. It takes time to go from a writer to a successful author. Enjoy the journey and never lose sight of the goal.

Ask for Help

An author by definition is an overworked, overstressed, overstimulated, creative human being. Sometimes you just need a hand. There are a thousand ways to get help. Would hiring a babysitter for a few hours a week give you time to create your platforms? Is there a friend with website development skills willing to help create your vision for your platform websites? Is there a college student in your life studying marketing and willing to do some market research for you? Do you have an associate or family member who knows how to make you laugh? Call them when you need a chuckle. Is there a mentor you can contact for encouragement? Do it.

Don't be afraid to ask for help. It doesn't mean you're failing or unable to do what's required to become successful. It simply means you're smart enough to reach out for answers or a well deserved diversion. Your support system might be other authors, family members or friends. Whoever they are, they want to help. Keeping yourself centered and focused is the name of the game when it comes to creating success.

You Can Do This!

Throughout this book, there were things you found easy, things you found difficult, and things you imagined to be down-right impossible. The trick is to remain steadfast in your plan. Use every tool you can find, read about or devise, because without focus you can easily lose your way. Once you drop the ball, it takes a lot of effort to regain what you may have lost. If you neglect posting to your blog for several months, it could take twice as many months and twice as many blogs to regain your readers. If you don't use Twitter or Facebook regularly, your friends and followers forget all about you. Asking for help, taking a moment to relax with friends and taking a moment to breathe can make all the difference in the world.

You can do this! And once you do, I look forward to picking up *The New York Times* and reading all about how you found your author success.

Appendix

TEN TOOLS FOR AUTHOR SUCCESS:
A QUICK REFERENCE HANDBOOK

The following is a brief overview of the ten most important tools for author success.

TOOL 1 – HAVE A PLAN

Your plan is the detail of how you will achieve your goals.

What are your goals? If this is your first book, what are your publisher's expectations? How do you propose to let the world know you have a book coming out and how do you intend to approach your market? In other words, what's your plan?

In order to create a competitive plan, you need competitive strategies. You can start by looking to your publisher. Ask them what they expect from your book. Which of their books, genres and authors are most successful and why?

Now, knowing what expectations your publisher has, you can multiply that and set a sales goal you'll be proud of. Within your goals should be the following categories:

Pre-launch exposure - How many pre-orders or prospective buyers do you want on a waiting list for your book? This will determine how active your pre-launch marketing and publicity will need to be.

First three months sales - Research the market, know standard sales numbers for your genre and how you're published, and make it BIGGER. A book's success or failure is based on its first quarter sales, don't sell yourself short. Set high goals and push for them.

Responses to your platform and social network elements - You'll have many platforms from which to shout about your book. Decide now how active you want the response rate to be on those platforms. This way you'll have viewing and response goals to reach. Of course, responses can only be made to a statement and you are the only one to make the statement, so knowing how active you want your prospective readers to be pretty much determines how proactive you are going to need to be within your platform elements.

Demand for the next book - Effective platforms and promotional efforts can create demand for more books from an author. Is this something you want? If so, add it to your goals list.

5 year sales goals - Look at your whole life, where do you want to be in five years? Does writing A LOT fit into that image? Do you want to use revenue earned from your books to improve your life? The sad truth is that most authors simply can't live on what they earn as writers, but with a plan, strategies and goals that are clear, you can create an income to substantially add to your dreams and lifestyle. It doesn't just happen. It must be set as a goal and made part of the plan.

Number of successful books in 10 years - Seriously think about this. Some writers see themselves as the author of one or two books, the creator of a mega success that rocks the world and then they can retire. There is a difference between fantasy, goals and strategic plans. Building a career demands you identify that career. If you want a booming writing career over 10 years, you may need to plan seven to ten books, several articles and short pieces published in collections, compilations or publications, speaking engagements, possibly writing in several genres or even adding non-fiction to your mix. This is a "going wide" strategy rather than a "going deep" strategy which limits the writer to a single genre or non-fiction subject. There are several industry theories on both approaches to building an author career, but the most important opinion is yours. You'll be living the career and doing the work.

Remember, you're not just an author; you're an author building a career. Once your goals are set, it's easy to take the following tools and put a plan in play.

TOOL 2 – FIND YOUR HOOKS

Your hooks are what makes you and your book special.

We've all taken a stroll through those huge book stores and gotten that shiver of terror. Even if you're already published and about to launch your second or tenth book, that fear trickles in and without warning you start to wonder. Who is going to buy my book when they're bombarded with all these other books? Yes, your writing is wonderful and your story kicks butt, but one twirl around and you see thousands of other author's offerings and can't help but feel the pressure. Bricks and mortar book store or online, it's the same.

Relax. The solution to the question is so simple it might shock you. The most important things you need to know to make your book stand out are not in marketing classrooms or genre statistics. They're not in publicity strategies or media hype. The most important elements to make you and your book stand apart are right inside your manuscript.

Your all important "hooks" are in your characters, your plot and your style. In other words, you have already created all the solutions you need to market, promote and publicize your book when you wrote the book.

What makes your book so special is what made your publisher sit up and take notice. Why ignore that for technical, expensive or professionally bought strategies when it's already mapped out for you? For example:

Location - Where does your book take place? Can you build, develop and implement entire promotions around that location?

Character - Is there something special about your characters? Are they werewolves? Historic sailors? Contemporary businessmen? Members of the club or organization that drives the story? Is there something special about your main character? Do they have a silly saying they repeat? Wear two different size shoes? Love cats? Enjoy root beer floats? Go deep, identify what makes your characters special and consider how that element might create a powerful "hook" that resonates with a prospective book buyer.

Association - If your main character is a gardener, are gardening clubs a good target? If he/she loves animals, are animal rescue groups a good readership target? Does your character connect with any large group of any profession or interest? Are these possible fans? Always consider association, it can open big doors for target marketing.

Plot - Is your book an adventure about whales or space travel or the end of time? Is your book a romance that involves people from different backgrounds? Is it a fantasy about supernatural characters struggling to remain hidden in the human world? Here are the facts about finding your "hooks" – they can be in any and every part of your book, they're implanted inside your story and they are ready to be effective.

The power of identifying all your possible hooks is that you can then find more target markets for your book. Automatically, readers of a specific genre will take a look and possibly buy the book. The trick to success is to go further and dig deeper to reach even more buyers.

TOOL 3 – BUILD YOUR PLATFORMS

Your platforms are what you stand on to tell people what you do and what you've accomplished.

Platforms are plural. If a politician stands on only one platform, he reaches only one set of ears. The same goes for an author. Your job is to reach as many sets of ears as possible, to reach them quickly, efficiently and with as little difficulty as possible.

What are your platforms?

Author Website (or blog) – This website (or blog) is specifically designed to promote you, the author. It will feature you, your books, your future projects and plans. It will offer insight to your future books and tell viewers what you're up to. This site will have a specific area for a Media Room where you'll list announcements about your various speaking and book events, upcoming interviews and links to videos or audio interviews you've already given. The Media Room will show all the press releases, have a downloadable bio and photo of the author, and contact information for the media. Even if your book is only e-published, you will use this website in a big way, creating as many avenues to promote all your work as you can, and connect with as many online readers as possible. E-published or traditionally published, your author website address should appear on your Twitter and Facebook profiles, email signatures, everywhere you can post it. This web presence is about all the author's work, published articles, short stories, all the books no matter genre and what the author's plans are for future books and all the news about his/her work.

Book Website – This website is very different. A Book Website is specifically designed to promote, market and expose a specific book or genre of books. For example, if you write romance, all of your romance (and sub-genre romance) books would have a showcase on your Romance Book Website. BUT, if you also write non-fiction about aviation, that would require a completely different book website. Why? Simple – these are two very different readers and a prospective book buyer will not explore a romance website for a book about landing gear, anymore than a reader wanting romance cares to explore a website about pilot qualifications. These two book websites should treat their specific audience differently and never cross reference to each other. IMPORTANT: an announcement about a book signing for your romance series would certainly be announced on your Author Website AND your Romance Book Website, but NOT on the Aviation Website. Also, an announcement about your speaking engagement to an aviation organization will appear on your Author Website AND your Aviation Book Website, but NOT on your Romance Website. Always respect and focus on the primary viewer of that particular website.

Author Expertise Blog – This can be as simple as an ongoing exploration of the research you did to write your book or are doing to write your next book. It can explore politics in your story and even talk about choices you made for the story. You can talk about character exploration and development, how you plot your books and where your ideas come from. You can use this blog to announce information about your promotions, and you can (and should) participate with other authors and guest blog on their blogs, announce their events on your blog and/or do interviews and reviews of your author friend's books. It's always wise to embed your author blog into your Author Platform website.

Character Blog – Not necessary but it's so much fun! This is a playful way of exploring your character/reader relationship dynamic. If your character is a curmudgeon and you develop a blog by him where he states his point of view and banters with the readers when they respond, you've made inroads into building loyalty and interest in the book. Obviously this doesn't work so well for non-fiction, unless you get very creative and invent a fictitious expert to state his feelings on the book. You'd be surprised how many readers respond to this approach and get involved with comments. If you're only e-published, this Character blog approach is very effective. Remember, an e-published book must reach e-readers, screen readers, and those fascinated with all things techie. Have fun with this, create impact and take your cues from the responses you get.

Twitter – Yes, you must Twitter. Create an account and build your followers carefully from a pool of possible book buyers, future fans, fellow authors, publishers, editors and agents. You will be amazed how much you can learn about the industry in your Twitter stream. Be active but be careful. Don't let it take you over. A good rule of thumb is to use Twitter at least twice a day for about 10-15 minutes each time. Interact, eavesdrop and comment on other follower's tweets, promote your blog and website updates, and always respond when someone talks to you. Efficient and effective tweeting is a learned skill and you'll soon discover that when done right, followers think you're there all the time and full of fun and valuable information even though you only tweet during a few breaks a day. I suggest you use a Twitter application as it helps you organize several streams of targets to follow, but you can do it any way that works best for you.

Facebook – There are several ways to use Facebook and I strongly suggest you Facebook every day. Not only are there different people on Facebook than Twitter, but they communicate differently. Without the Twitter limitation of 140 characters to make a point, Facebook creates several venues of communications. Everything from your current status and direct messaging, tagging and inviting friends to join events or joining groups targeted to your book are all there. Facebook every day with something interactive in your status. Build friends by reaching out and asking for friends but be careful what kind of friends you make. If you want to talk about the subject of your book which is about murder investigation techniques, you should have very few baker friends or friends who love scrap booking. Be sensible and be targeted with all your efforts. A downfall at Facebook can be the numerous social games and game forums. Choose how you want to spend your Facebook time, be practical and efficient because as writers and authors, we really need to protect our writing time. Do NOT mix your personal Facebook activities with your book Facebook activities. In other words, keep those accounts separate.

Email – Email lists: we have them, several of them in fact. We build them almost daily but what we seldom do is categorize them to make them easy to use. Create a group list for people you know who would love your book, love to read your blog updates, love to know what's happening with your book or love to hear about your next project. It's likely that if you explore the massive contact list your already have, you can find many people to fall under this group category. Create the group and voila, you've made one more contact to take one more person to your blog or your Book Website Media Page or invite to your book launch party. You've created one more venue for helping your author friends promote their books when you announce you've done a blog tour interview for them, and you've opened an opportunity for the receivers of your emails to pass them further to their friends and followers interested in your genre. Email. Right there under our nose. I'm sure if you think about it, you can find several ways to create email lists and use them to streamline promotional and marketing strategies.

Online Groups/Organizations – You can find them on LinkedIn, Facebook, Twitter, Yahoo Groups, anywhere! These groups can work as support for your writing efforts, or serve as association groups to promote your book. It takes a bit to find them and decide how they'll work for you, but this is worth the effort. Be a joiner but don't overdo it. Remember, participate only in the groups that not only are interesting to you, but serve your efforts as well. If you do join, really make an effort to participate. Get into the discussions, especially if this is an interest group that pertains to your book plot or non-fiction subject. Never imagine that simply joining anything – a group, Twitter, Facebook, LinkedIn, Yahoo private groups and/or organizations – means automatic sales. It simply means that you've opened your possible audience. You're doing it in a protected environment and many groups will slap your wrist if all you do is promote, promote, promote. You need to seriously participate in the groups, give and get support and that's what turns into book sales.

Live Networking – With all the online and internet hubbub, we often forget our real life, living, breathing network. Your family, work friends, church. Your dentist, vet, eye doctor. The health club, the woman who cuts your hair or the massage therapist you use. Don't forget about where your kids go to school, where you shop for groceries and where you get your lottery tickets. These are breathing people who know you already. These are people who like you. Most people know few authors and are thrilled to know one. They become excited walking, talking advertisements for your book. Don't leave this vital network out of your loop, whether you write fiction or non-fiction, are traditionally published or e-published, remember to toot your horn to everyone you know. Remember though, not everyone will support you in the way you think they will. Some will buy your book, some won't. Some will shout your success to the world, others will find faults. Whatever their reactions and reasons are, respect them and never force yourself on people. If they want to help you, they will. And if they don't - well - there's not much you can do about it except to forget it and move on to those who do support you.

TOOL 4 – UNDERSTAND YOUR MARKET

Understanding your market is research.

What other authors write in your genres? Where can one buy their book? Are you e-published? Who else is e-published and successful? What are some of the best promotions or marketing efforts you've seen for a book? Do book videos work for your genre? Do you understand how the most successful authors manage their careers?

I'm sure you can come up with a hundred more questions about your market as well. It's vital to ask the questions, explore what other authors are doing, what works and doesn't work and how far "wide" or "deep" they go with their marketing strategies.

Don't just look at the publishing industry either. Look around. Everything you buy is being marketed and promoted. What kind of promotions make an impact for you? Can that approach work for your book?

Next, where is your market? If you're e-publishing, your buyer is on the computer. Exploration for ways to reach them goes further than simply using your platforms, you have to reach them at their platforms. When you read an interesting blog, respond to it. Comment. Become known to the author and they will frequent your blog too. (If one of your hooks is dog lovers, you need to connect with dog lovers online. They have blogs. You can respond because you like dogs. After all, there's a dog lover in your book.) Use all the promotional options open for authors; blog tours, interviews, book reviews.

If you're both traditionally published and e-published, never forget to find your prospective buyer through your hooks. If you don't know who will want your book, how can you talk to them?

TOOL 5 – PUBLICITY

Publicity is using the media to create relevant exposure for your book.

Take a serious look at your book, especially your hooks - those unique elements that not only make your book stand apart, but identify additional readers for your book beyond genre followers. What in your book or connected to your hook might lend itself to publicity or a charity? Connecting with a charity does several wonderful things. It shows you're a caring author, it supports something you care about, and it connects with your story.

Don't just randomly choose a charity. If your book has nothing to do with cancer research and none of the characters are cancer survivors, it's not really productive to connect your book with that charity. If the charity is near and dear to your heart, by all means support it, but don't connect it to your book, it will look and feel random.

If, on the other hand your story or non-fiction subject does directly connect with a charity, move ahead. Create fundraising events. Donate a portion of your book profits to the charity and make sure they know. Be sure to have the charity logo displayed with an announcement that a portion of your profits support Cancer Research, or The Kidney Foundation, or the ASPCA or whichever charity works.

It's a kind of giving back that is good for the author's soul and good for the book buyer's soul. And, as long as you are doing well, the charity will notify its supporters that you are doing this. It just may result in more sales.

Be honest about this, no fake or half efforts. Charitable organizations all over the world are desperate for financial help. It's a chance for the author to be a hero.

All of this takes place in the world of the media. Press releases and press contacts are a huge part of your publicity, and the charity will benefit from this press as well. Remember the Media Room in your Author Platform website? This is the kind of information that goes in there. If a newspaper does a story about your charity fundraising event, you post that story. If you are interviewed and/or a podcast is created, you post it in your Media Room. News doesn't just happen, you have to make it happen.

TOOL 6 – YOUR IMAGE

Your image is what you present to the world.

No Facebook or Twitter avatars your mother would be embarrassed to see. No pictures of your dog or cat cleaning itself. No photos of you drunk at a club, whooping it up. You're an author, be aware of your image. This doesn't require a professional photo session with an expensive photographer, just a nice picture of you, clean and neat. We don't need to see you working hard at the computer or appearing overly serious. You can show your personality, smile, enjoy the moment. Just remember, literary agents, publishers, other authors and your prospective book buyers are looking at that avatar. Are you really proud of it?

If you prefer not to use a photo of yourself, your book cover is a good option. No book cover yet? Use an image that represents your book until you have one. And one final suggestion, please don't change your avatar picture more than once a year. It's how your friends and followers recognize you. Don't confuse us.

TOOL 7 – MARKETING

Marketing is building awareness that your book exists.
An author's marketing tools are:

- Your Polished Image
- Your Platforms Activity
- Your Social Networking

Sounds a little like everything, doesn't it? But everything thus far was put together just to build awareness of you and your book. If you don't blog regularly, use social media effectively and on a regular basis, keep your websites updated and Media Room neat and full with every element readily downloadable for the media to use, you've dropped the ball. Only with all these things in play and working like a perfectly oiled machine, can you know that you've done your job and created awareness for your coming book. If you haven't, all your promotional efforts will fall on deaf ears. Sad but true.

TOOL 8 – PROMOTION

Promotion is the activity around which you sell your book.

It's finally time to promote that book about which you've been writing, talking, blogging, Facebooking and Tweeting about. Time to promote the book to all those prospective readers you've been reaching out to. Remember all those goals listed under Tool #1? Now you can make them happen.

The question is how to promote? Again, it's all inside your manuscript. Create promotions and events that are so tightly related to your subject focus, story and characters you can hear it squeak. If the murder in your mystery takes place in a museum, hold your book launch events and speaking engagements in museums or museum gift stores. Find the hook"and twist it tightly to make it your promotional key. Is your main character a coffee expert? Have your events in coffee shops, use coffee shop discount coupons as bookmarks, campaign to have a coffee drink at the coffee shop named after your book. Does your story involve a corrupt lawyer poaching wild animals in Africa? Hold your events at the zoo and have tee shirts that say "So Zoo Me!"

E-published? Again, there are perfect venues for your promotions. The zoo has a website. So does the museum and the coffee shop. They might be thrilled to let you show your book on that website, perhaps sell your book with a link on that website, especially if you're donating a portion of your profits to support the zoo or museum or a charity near and dear to the coffee shop's heart.

Get creative. Seek every opportunity and promote! And by the way, don't forget the simplest and most effective way to promote: just tell people! Tell all those friends on Facebook and Twitter that your book is now available and where they can buy it. Let all your associates in those online and live groups know that the book is out, and remember to get the news out to your email groups too.

TOOL 9 – RESOURCES REQUIRED

Understandably, few authors can afford everything they want in the line of services. Some expenses are vital, like the cost of a good editor and cover designer if you're self published. Choose carefully for other services. If you can't build your own websites and can't afford to hire someone to build them for you, think about trading a service. Be careful not to juggle too many things at once, a writer can't write if all his time is spent chatting on Twitter or bartering with friends. Use careful time management, if not, it will cost you in the long run, possibly a career, because no one cares about an author who never finishes a book.

When looking at services from professionals, beware of the "free" services that pop into your email inbox. We both know nothing is ever free and if it is, it's usually worthless. Another thing we all know is that there are no shortcuts, so don't leap to pay someone to make you a top ten best seller in four short weeks. It won't happen.

Be careful of the promotional item sellers. You may not need tee shirts or printed coffee mugs or ink pens with your book's name on them. Think before you order.

Be picky, have a plan and don't let some sparkly, crazy silliness come along and take you away from your plan. If tee shirts were on your original plan for a good reason, because they work with your book's hook and make sense, then order them.

Always be reasonable. Does the tee short have to be 100% organic cotton? Does the book video have to be produced by a Hollywood director? Does your book promotion really require real actors in period costume to appear at your launch party? Only you can decide.

Create a budget and STICK TO IT, even if that budget is zero.

TOOL 10 – FOLLOW UP

Consistency builds a career. Don't drop a ball anywhere – not in your platforms, not in your social marketing or blogging or group associations. Don't simply drop off the planet for a while, you will pay when it comes time to rebuild your lost following.

If you are an expert at something as part of your platforms, be the expert, always and everywhere. Expect people to ask questions and plan to answer them. Be gracious.

Constantly look for new growth avenues, new opportunities to make yourself and your book(s) visible. New places and audiences to sell your book to.

And finally, keep your Book Business Plan alive, well, growing and breathing! If you take care of it, it will take care of you and your career.

ABOUT THE AUTHOR

Deborah Riley-Magnus is an author and an Author Success Coach. She has a twenty-seven year professional background in marketing, advertising and public relations as a writer for print, television and radio. She writes fiction in several genres as well as non-fiction. She's lived on both the east and west coast of the United States and has traveled the country widely.

Having lived, worked and written in Los Angeles for many years, she recently returned to her hometown of Pittsburgh.

ACKNOWLEDGMENTS

Natalie Preston, my reader and logic checker. My wonderful publisher, Michelle Halket. All the authors who shared their experiences with me and all the authors and industry pros who tried and tested the suggestions in this book, Pamela DuMond, Lisette Brodey, K.M. Weiland, David Rozansky, Marc Nash, David Bowman, Carol Silvis, Heikki Hietala, Angela Slatter, Amy Grech, Aurora Lightbourne, M.M. Bennetts, Sascha Illyvich, Keta Diablo, Suzanne Fyhrie-Parrott, Moriah Jovan, Ruth Hartman, Jeremy C. Shipp, Melinda B. Pierce, Joan LeMont, Meg Mims, Tara Lain, and so many more.

And finally, all the authors, writers and publishing industry professionals who asked the questions that spurred me to find and develop author marketing solutions for a new publishing era.

USEFUL READING

The Artist's Way; Julia Cameron

How to Write a Book Proposal; Michael Larsen

Guerilla Marketing for Writers; J. Conrad Levinson, Rick Frishman and Michael Larsen

Guerilla PR; Michael Levine

Guerilla Publicity; J. Conrad Levinson, Rick Frishman and Jill Lublin

Positioning, The Battle for your Mind; Al Ries and Jack Trout

The Sell Your Novel Tool Kit; Elizabeth Lyon

The Zen of Social Media Marketing; Shama Kabani and Chris Brogan

Six Thinking Hats; Edward De Bono

CPSIA information can be obtained at www.ICGtesting.com
Printed in the USA
BVOW082357110612

292355BV00002B/1/P